LANGENSCHEIDT-LEKTÜRE 67

MURDER! MURDER? MURDER!

ENGLISCH

4	**Strange Adventures**	Abenteuergeschichten, die sich besonderer Beliebtheit erfreuen.
13	**13 Whodunits**	Kriminalgeschichten u.a. von Agatha Christie, O. Henry und Saki.
15	**Laugh and Be Merry!**	Köstlicher britischer Humor in Short Stories und Witzen.
42	**Short Stories**	Ausgesuchte Erzählungen, die sich durch ihren hervorragenden Stil auszeichnen.
60	**Humorous Short Stories**	Spaßige Situationskomik und amüsante Schlaglichter auf englische Originalität.
61	**The Birds/Kiss Me Again, Stranger**	Hier – die Vorlage für Hitchcocks Thriller, dazu ein weiterer Shocker.
66	**A Steinbeck Reader**	Drei Kurzgeschichten des großen amerikanischen Erzählers.
67	**Murder! Murder? Murder!**	Vier Mordgeschichten und vier ungewöhnliche Täter – besonders spannende Lektüren.
70	**So spricht der Amerikaner!**	Eine kleine Einführung in das Amerikanische Englisch.
71	**Spotlights**	15 englische und amerikanische Kurzgeschichten.
72	**Scoundrels**	Zwei leichte englische Kurzgeschichten.

FRANZÖSISCH

44	**Nouvelles françaises**	Eine Sammlung literarisch interessanter französischer Novellen.
57	**Textes français modernes**	Humoristische und ernste „Auskünfte" über historische und kulturgeschichtliche Themen.
59	**Images de la France**	Französische Texte über Land und Leute.
62	**Thanatos Palace Hotel**	Novellistische Kostbarkeiten, wie sie nur aus der Feder André Maurois' fließen können.
68	**Humour à gogo**	Typische Witze sind in diesem Lektüreband mit humorvollen Kurzgeschichten vereinigt.

ITALIENISCH

7	**Un po' di tutto**	Aktuelle Einblicke in die Verhältnisse des Landes und in das Geistesleben des Volkes.
69	**Storie poliziesche**	Moderne italienische Kriminalgeschichten – sie halten den Leser bis zur letzten Seite gefangen.

RUSSISCH

55	**Moderne russische Erzählungen**	Typische Kurzgeschichten, teils humoristisch, teils ernst.
56	**Leichte russische Kurzgeschichten**	Populäre Aufsätze, Anekdoten, Sprichwörter und Kurzgeschichten.

SPANISCH

36	**Cuentos Españoles**	Charakteristische Erzählungen aus dem spanischen Volksleben.
58	**Lecturas amenas**	Humorvolle Erzählungen in spanischer Umgangssprache.
65	**Rodando por España**	Interessante Einblicke in das Alltagsleben des spanischen Volkes.

Langenscheidt-Lektüre 67

Murder! Murder? Murder!

Fünf Mordgeschichten und fünf ungewöhnliche Täter

von Dorothy Sayers, Edgar Allan Poe, K.R.G. Browne und G.D.H. u. M.Cole

LANGENSCHEIDT
BERLIN · MÜNCHEN · WIEN · ZÜRICH

Auflage:	*13.*	*12.*	*11.*	*10.*	*9.*	*Letzte Zahlen*
Jahr:	*1995*	*94*	*93*	*92*	*91*	*maßgeblich*

Druck: Druckhaus Langenscheidt, Berlin-Schöneberg
Printed in Germany · ISBN 3-468-44670-5

Vorwort

Die fünf Erzählungen dieses Bandes sind keine Kriminalgeschichten im üblichen Sinne. Es sind zwar „Mordgeschichten", aber die vorliegende Auswahl zeigt, daß es nicht immer nur Detektive und Kriminalbeamte sein müssen, die für die zusätzliche Spannung sorgen. Zwar bleibt die Fragestellung „Wer ist der Schuldige?", aber weniger Motiv und Tat als vielmehr die Persönlichkeit von Täter und Opfer stehen im Vordergrund jeder dieser ungewöhnlichen Geschichten.

Zwei Autoren schienen uns für diesen Band besonders geeignet zu sein, Dorothy L. Sayers und Edgar Allan Poe: Dorothy Sayers – neben Agatha Christie wohl die bedeutendste Autorin von Kriminalromanen in England – weil sie von jeher bemüht war, durch überzeugende Charaktere die Mechanisierung des Detektivromans zu überwinden; Edgar Allan Poe, weil er als Vorläufer des heutigen logisch deduzierenden Kriminalromans kriminalistischen Scharfblick mit dem Hang zum Phantastischen und Unheimlichen verbindet. Dorothy Sayers sagt über Poe und die Etablierung des Kriminalromans als Literaturgattung: „The ball – the original nucleus deposited by Edgar Allan Poe . . . – was at last set rolling. As it went, it swelled into a vast mass – it set off others – it became a spate – a torrent – an avalanche of mystery fiction."

Aber auch Humor und englischer Spleen kommen in zwei Geschichten anderer Autoren zu Wort. Alles in allem, wie wir hoffen, eine gelungene Mischung spannender Geschichten aus dem reichen Schatz dieser Literaturgattung.

Der vorliegende Band bringt für die Übersetzungshilfen eine Besonderheit. Wörter, die in der Vokabelspalte enthalten sind, werden im laufenden Text mit einem kleinen Kreis gekennzeichnet. Der Leser erspart sich dadurch vergebliches Suchen. Er kommt schneller voran.

LANGENSCHEIDT

Inhaltsverzeichnis

Erklärung der Aussprachebezeichnung

A. Vokale und Diphthonge

[ɑː] reines langes a, wie in Vater, kam, Schwan: *far* [fɑː], *father* [ˈfɑːðə].

[ʌ] kommt im Deutschen nicht vor. Kurzes dunkles a, bei dem die Lippen nicht gerundet sind. Vorn und offen gebildet: *butter* [ˈbʌtə], *come* [kʌm], *colour* [ˈkʌlə], *blood* [blʌd], *flourish* [ˈflʌriʃ], *twopence* [ˈtʌpəns].

[æ] heller, ziemlich offener, nicht zu kurzer Laut. Raum zwischen Zunge und Gaumen noch größer als bei ä in Ähre: *fat* [fæt], *man* [mæn].

[ɛə] nicht zu offenes halblanges ä; im Englischen nur vor r, das als ein dem ä nachhallendes ə erscheint: *bare* [bɛə], *pair* [pɛə], *there* [ðɛə].

[ai] Bestandteile: helles, zwischen ɑː und æ liegendes a und schwächeres offenes i. Die Zunge hebt sich halbwegs zur i-Stellung: *I* [ai], *lie* [lai], *dry* [drai].

[au] Bestandteile: helles, zwischen ɑː und æ liegendes a und schwächeres offenes u: *house* [haus], *now* [nau].

[ei] halboffenes e, nach i auslautend, indem die Zunge sich halbwegs zur i-Stellung hebt: *date* [deit], *play* [plei], *obey* [əˈbei].

[e] halboffenes kurzes e, etwas geschlossener als das e in Bett: *bed* [bed], *less* [les].

[ə] flüchtiger Gleitlaut, ähnlich dem deutschen, flüchtig gesprochenen e in Gelage: *about* [əˈbaut], *butter* [ˈbʌtə], *connect* [kəˈnekt].

[əu] mit [ə] beginnend und in schwaches u auslautend; keine Rundung der Lippen, kein Heben der Zunge: *note* [nəut], *boat* [bəut], *below* [biˈləu].

[iː] langes i, wie in lieb, Bibel, aber etwas offener einsetzend als im Deutschen; wird in Südengland doppellautig gesprochen, indem sich die Zunge allmählich zur i-Stellung hebt: *scene* [siːn], *sea* [siː], *feet* [fiːt], *ceiling* [ˈsiːliŋ].

[i] kurzes offenes i wie in bin, mit: *big* [big], *city* [ˈsiti].

[iə] halboffenes halblanges i mit nachhallendem ə: *here* [hiə], *hear* [hiə], *inferior* [inˈfiəriə].

[ɔː] offener langer, zwischen a und o schwebender Laut: *fall* [fɔːl], *nought* [nɔːt], *or* [ɔː], *before* [biˈfɔː].

[ɔ] offener kurzer, zwischen a und o schwebender Laut, offener als das o in Motte: *god* [gɔd], *not* [nɔt], *wash* [wɔʃ], *hobby* [ˈhɔbi].

[ɔi] Bestandteile: offenes o und schwächeres offenes i. Die Zunge hebt sich halbwegs zur i-Stellung: *voice* [vɔis], *boy* [bɔi], *annoy* [əˈnɔi].

[əː] im Deutschen fehlender Laut; offenes langes ö, etwa wie gedehnt gesprochenes ö in öffnen, Mörder; kein Vorstülpen oder Runden der Lippen; kein Heben der Zunge: *word* [wəːd], *girl* [gəːl], *learn* [ləːn], *murmur* [ˈməːmə].

[uː] langes u wie in Buch, doch ohne Lippenrundung; vielfach diphthongisch als halboffenes langes u mit nachhallendem geschlossenem u: *fool* [fuːl], *shoe* [ʃuː], *you* [juː], *rule* [ruːl], *canoe* [kəˈnuː].

[uə] halboffenes halblanges u mit nachhallendem ə: *poor* [puə], *sure* [ʃuə], *allure* [əˈljuə].

[u] flüchtiges u: *put* [put], *look* [luk], *careful* [ˈkɛəful].

Ganz vereinzelt werden auch die folgenden französischen Laute gebraucht: Die Nasale [ɑ̃] wie in frz. *blanc*, [ɔ̃] wie in frz. *bonbon* und [ɛ̃] wie in frz. *vin*, sowie die drei Vokale [o] wie in frz. *chaud*, [ɛ] wie in frz. *belle* und [ø] wie in frz. *monsieur*.

Die **Länge eines Vokals** wird durch [ː] bezeichnet, z. B. *ask* [ɑːsk], *astir* [əˈstəː]. Die **Betonung** der englischen Wörter wird durch das Zeichen [ˈ] vor der zu betonenden Silbe angegeben, z. B. *onion* [ˈʌnjən].

B. Konsonanten

[r] nur vor Vokalen gesprochen. Völlig verschieden vom deutschen Zungenspitzen- oder Zäpfchen-r. Die Zungenspitze bildet mit der oberen Zahnwulst eine Enge, durch die der Ausatmungsstrom mit Stimmton hindurchgetrieben wird, ohne den Laut zu rollen. Am Ende eines Wortes wird r nur bei Bindung mit dem Anlautvokal des folgenden Wortes gesprochen: *rose* [rəuz], *pride* [praid], *there is* [ðɛərˈiz].

[ʒ] stimmhaftes sch, wie g in Genie, j in Journal: *azure* [ˈæʒə], *jazz* [dʒæz], *jeep* [dʒiːp], *large* [lɑːdʒ].

[ʃ] stimmloses sch, wie im Deutschen Schnee, rasch: *shake* [ʃeik], *washing* [ˈwɔʃiŋ], *lash* [læʃ].

[θ] im Deutschen nicht vorhandener stimmloser Lispellaut; durch Anlegen der Zunge an die oberen Schneidezähne hervorgebracht: *thin* [θin], *path* [pɑːθ], *method* [ˈmeθəd].

[ð] derselbe Laut stimmhaft, d.h. mit Stimmton: *there* [ðɛə], *breathe* [briːð], *father* [ˈfɑːðə].

[s] stimmloser Zischlaut, entsprechend dem deutschen ß in Spaß, reißen: *see* [siː], *hats* [hæts], *decide* [diˈsaid].

[z] stimmhafter Zischlaut wie im Deutschen sausen: *zeal* [ziːl], *rise* [raiz], *horizon* [həˈraizn].

[ŋ] wird wie der deutsche Nasenlaut in fangen, singen gebildet: *ring* [riŋ], *singer* [ˈsiŋə].

[ŋk] derselbe Laut mit nachfolgendem k wie im Deutschen senken, Wink: *ink* [iŋk], *tinker* [ˈtiŋkə].

[w] flüchtiges, mit Lippe an Lippe gesprochenes w, aus der Mundstellung für uː gebildet: *will* [wil], *swear* [swɛə], *queen* [kwiːn].

[f] stimmloser Lippenlaut wie im Deutschen flott: *fat* [fæt], *tough* [tʌf], *effort* [ˈefət].

[v] stimmhafter Lippenlaut wie im Deutschen Vase, Ventil: *vein* [vein], *velvet* [ˈvelvit].

[j] flüchtiger zwischen j und i schwebender Laut: *onion* [ˈʌnjən], *yes* [jes], *filial* [ˈfiljəl].

Verwandte Abkürzungen

° vor einem englischen Wort im Text zeigt an, daß dieses Wort in der Vokabelspalte übersetzt wird.

Abkzg	Abkürzung
AE	amerikanisches Englisch
BE	britisches Englisch
bes.	besonders
e–e	eine
e–r	einer
e–s	eines
et.	etwas
F	Familiär (= Umgangssprache)
j–d	jemand
j–m	jemandem
j–n	jemanden
j–s	jemandes
m–e	meine
m–r	meiner
m–s	meines
od., *od.*	oder
o.s.	oneself
Pl	Plural
s–e	seine
s–r	seiner
s–s	seines
Sg	Singular
sl.	Slang
s.o.	someone
s.th.	something
u.	und

Wir danken den folgenden Verlagen und Agenturen für Abdrucksgenehmigungen:

Elek Books Ltd und David Higham Associates, Ltd für „The Fountain Plays“ von Dorothy L. Sayers (aus der Sammlung „Murder Mixture“).

Curtis Brown Ltd für „A Lesson in Crime“ von G. D. H. und M. Cole.

Through The Window

BY K. R. G. BROWNE

At the corner by Lord's °Cricket Ground I paused to °light a cigarette and °give thanks to Providence °for my lack of a wife. For the hour—if the clock above the Underground station was to be believed—was four-fifteen of a °bright June morning, and I was °homeward bound from an evening which had begun well with a °regimental dinner and ended °riotously with a poker-party in Bat Farquhar's flat. An evening of wine, °reminiscence, anecdote and song—an evening, °in short, such as your °Benedict °enjoys only °at the risk of °subsequent °domestic °tribulation. But I, being no woman's °chattel, had no reason to °dread the future or °rack my brains for °incredible excuses; and though—like every man—I was not without my own particular and private °troubles, at the moment these °weighed upon me not at all, for I was in that °mellow °frame of mind which comes of an °admirable meal, much good °discourse and a °measure of luck °with the cards. And so it was that, as I crossed the road and °plunged into the °decorous °byways of St. John's Wood, I was °constrained to sing a little, °by way of welcome to the dawn.

And why not? If a man may not sing on his way home from a regimen-

cricket ground ['krikit graund] *Kricketplatz*
light [lait] *anzünden*
give thanks to providence [giv θæŋks, 'prɔvidəns] *der Vorsehung danken*
... for my lack of a wife [læk, waif] *dafür, daß ich keine (Ehe)Frau habe*
bright [brait] *strahlend*
homeward bound ['həumwəd baund] *auf dem Heimweg*
regimental dinner [redʒi'mentl 'dinə] *hier: Essen m-s Regimentes*
riotous ['raiətəs] *ausgelassen*
reminiscence [remi'nisns] *Erinnerung*
in short [ʃɔːt] *kurz(um)*
benedict ['benidikt] = benedick ['benedik] *frischgebackener Ehemann*
enjoy [in'dʒɔi] *genießen*
at the risk of [risk] *unter der Gefahr*
subsequent ['sʌbsikwənt] *folgend, später*
domestic [dəu'mestik] *häuslich*
tribulation [tribju'leiʃən] *Leiden*
chattel ['tʃætl] *Sklave*
dread [dred] *fürchten*
rack one's brains [ræk, breinz] *sich den Kopf zermartern*
incredible [in'kredəbl] *unglaubhaft*
trouble ['trʌbl] *Schwierigkeit*
weigh upon [wei] *hier: belasten*
mellow F ['meləu] *heiter*
frame of mind [freim, maind] *Gemütsverfassung, -zustand*
admirable ['ædmərəbl] *großartig*
discourse [dis'kɔːs] *Gespräch*
measure of luck ['meʒə, lʌk] *Portion Glück*
with the cards [kɑːdz] *beim Kartenspiel*
plunge into [plʌndʒ] *stürmen in, plötzlich betreten*

tal dinner, when may he sing? I would not have it thought, °mind you, that I sang loudly in a °raucous voice, to the °discomfort of the neighbourhood. Not so. I sang softly in a gentlemanly °tenor, robbing no man of his rest. °As for the °purport of my song, °that is neither here nor there; it is enough to say that it was a ballad of the kind that may °with impunity be sung at dawn in St. John's Wood, or at high noon in the Sahara, or at midnight in Alaska, but never in a °drawing-room at tea-time by one °having a regard for the conventions. A manly and comforting song, if you °follow me, but °somewhat °limited in its °appeal.

It was as I °embarked upon the eleventh and °penultimate verse of this song that I °turned the corner into °Laburnum Road, N.W. 8, and saw before me a policeman. And °at sight of that large blue shape my song °perished suddenly within me, for there is something about policemen that °paralyses my °vocal cords, even after a regimental dinner and a measure of luck with the cards.

This was a very high, very broad, very °efficient-looking policeman, and he stood upon the °kerb near the corner, rocking gently back and forth upon his heels and °gazing °pensively into °infinity, as policemen will when there are no murderers or °motorists °available for their °diversion. As I approached, he turned slowly and °surveyed me °in a mildly interested way, °much as a °naturalist might survey a °beetle of whose exact °species

decorous [ˈdekərəs] *(wohl-) anständig*
byway [ˈbaiwei] *Nebenstraße*
be constrained to do s.th. [kənˈstreind] *sich gezwungen fühlen, et. zu tun*
by way of *in der Absicht zu*

---

mind you *wohlgemerkt!*
raucous [ˈrɔːkəs] *rauh, heiser*
discomfort [disˈkʌmfət] *Verdruß*
tenor [ˈtenə] *Tenor(stimme)*
as for *was ... betrifft*
purport [ˈpəːpət] *Inhalt, Sinn*
that is neither here nor there [ˈnaiðə, nɔː] *das gehört nicht zur Sache*
with impunity [imˈpjuːniti] *ungestraft*
drawing-room [ˈdrɔiŋrum] *Salon*
have a regard for the conventions [riˈgɑːd, kənˈvenʃənz] *auf Sitte* od. *Konventionen Rücksicht nehmen*
follow [ˈfɔləu] *verstehen*
somewhat [ˈsʌmwɔt] *etwas*
limited [ˈlimitid] *begrenzt*
appeal [əˈpiːl] *Anklang, Wirkung*
embark upon [imˈbɑːk] *anfangen*
penultimate [piˈnʌltimit] *vorletzt*
turn the corner into [təːn, ˈkɔːnə] *um die (Straßen-) Ecke einbiegen in*
laburnum [ləˈbəːnəm] *Goldregen*
at sight of [sait] *beim Anblick*
perish [ˈperiʃ] *zugrunde gehen, sterben*
paralyse [ˈpærəlaiz] *lähmen*
vocal cords *Pl* [ˈvəukəl kɔːdz] *Stimmbänder*
efficient-looking [iˈfiʃəntˈlukiŋ] *tüchtig aussehend*
kerb BE [kəːb] *Bordstein*
gaze [geiz] *starren*
pensive [ˈpensiv] *nachdenklich*
infinity [inˈfiniti] *Unendliche*
motorist [ˈməutərist] *Autofahrer*
available [əˈveiləbl] *anwesend*
diversion [daiˈvəːʃən] *Zeitvertreib, Unterhaltung*

he was a little °doubtful. I °observed that he had a °keen blue eye and very red hair and a chin like the toe of a football boot; and I °noted also that he was a °comparatively °juvenile policeman, being of my own age or °thereabouts.

Now, °ordinarily it is not my °way to °engage policemen in conversation. My °conscience is as °tranquil as that of the °average man, but policemen °awe me, because they are such °lofty folk. I myself am of no great °stature, and it is somehow °humiliating to have to lean back and talk up at a man, after the °fashion of a tourist examining the Eiffel Tower. But on this morning, °as it happened, I was °feeling conversationally inclined, for I will not °deny that good wine has the °effect of °unshackling my tongue, as any of my °relations would be only too willing to °testify. And it seemed to me, too, that this was a rather °bored and melancholy policeman, and that it was my °plain duty as a °taxpaying °citizen to °cheer him with a kindly word. Nothing on earth, you understand, would have °induced me to °sing to him, but °mere courtesy °forbade me to °pass him by without a word of greeting.

'Good morning, °officer,' I said, having heard somewhere that it °gratifies a policeman to be so °addressed.

'Good morning,' answered the policeman; and if he was gratified, he did not show it.

'I've been to a party,' I said—not meaning to °boast, but with °intent to

survey [sə:ˈvei] *mustern*
in a mildly interested way [ˈmaildli, ˈintristid, wei] *mit nachsichtig-freundlichem Interesse*
much [mʌtʃ] *ungefähr, etwa*
naturalist [ˈnætʃrəlist] *Zoologe*
beetle [ˈbi:tl] *Käfer*
species [ˈspi:ʃi:z] *Art, Spezies*

---

doubtful [ˈdautful] *unsicher*
observe [əbˈzə:v] *beobachten*
keen [ki:n] *scharf*
note [nəut] *bemerken*
comparatively [kəmˈpærətivli] *verhältnismäßig, ziemlich*
juvenile [ˈdʒu:vinail] *jung*
thereabouts [ˈðεərəbauts] *so etwa*
ordinarily [ˈɔ:dnrili] *gewöhnlich*
way *Art*
engage s.o. in conversation [inˈgeidʒ, kɔnvəˈseiʃən] *j-n ins Gespräch ziehen*
conscience [ˈkɔnʃəns] *Gewissen*
tranquil [ˈtræŋkwil] *ruhig*
average man [ˈævəridʒ mæn] *Durchschnittsbürger*
awe [ɔ:] *einschüchtern*
lofty [ˈlɔfti] *hochaufragend*
stature [ˈstætʃə] *Statur*
humiliating [hju:ˈmilieitiŋ] *demütigend*
fashion [ˈfæʃən] *Art u. Weise*
as it happens [ˈhæpənz] *wie es sich so trifft*
feel conversationally inclined [fi:l, kɔnvəˈseiʃnəli, inˈklaind] *hier: nach Unterhaltung zumute sein*
deny [diˈnai] *leugnen*
effect [iˈfekt] *Wirkung*
unshackle [ˈʌnˈʃækl] *befreien, hier: lösen*
relation [riˈleiʃən] *Verwandte; Verwandtschaft*
testify [ˈtestifai] *bezeugen*
bored [bɔ:d] *gelangweilt*
plain [plein] *einfach, eindeutig*
taxpaying [ˈtækspeiiŋ] *steuerzahlend*
citizen [ˈsitizn] *Bürger*
cheer [tʃiə] *aufheitern*
induce [inˈdju:s] *bewegen*
sing to s.o. [siŋ] *j-m vorsingen*
mere courtesy [miə ˈkə:tisi] *pure Höflichkeit*

explain my presence in Laburnum Road at four-twenty of a bright June morning.

°'Is that so?' said the policeman; and he looked thoughtfully at my °shirt-front, whereon Bat Farquhar —ever a °humorous °lad—°had seen fit to °work out certain °monetary problems with the help of an °indelible pencil. °Boys will be boys, and who am I to °deny a friend his little harmless pleasures?

'They're being worn like that now, °you know,' I said °coughing °slightly, and drawing my coat about me. 'A °jolly day, don't you think?'

'Yes,' said the policeman.

It was becoming clear to me that this was not one of our more °chatty policemen, but I thought no less of him °on that account, for a night °spent on the °beat in Laburnum Road would °atrophy any man's °powers of conversation.

'Well,' I said, °keeping the ball rolling, 'thanks very much for °looking after Laburnum Road so nicely. It's a great °comfort to know that I can °go out any time and—'

'You °live in this road?' said the policeman.

'I can't deny it,' I answered. 'At Number Twenty. Any time you're °passing—'

'Ah,' said the policeman. 'Then do you know who lives in that house over there?' And he °pointed to a house that °faced us across the road; an °excessively °neat little house in a °painfully neat little garden; a °smug

forbade [fəˈbæd] *von* forbid [fəˈbid] *verbieten*
pass by [pɑːs] *vorbeigehen an*
officer [ˈɔfisə] *Herr Wachtmeister!*
gratify [ˈgrætifai] *erfreuen*
address [əˈdres] *anreden*
boast [bəust] *prahlen, großtun*
intent [inˈtent] *Absicht*

---

is that so? *wirklich?*
shirt-front [ˈʃəːtfrʌnt] *Hemdbrust*
humorous [ˈhjuːmərəs] *lustig komisch, humorvoll*
lad [læd] *Bursche, Junge*
had seen fit [siːn fit] *von* see fit [siː] *es für richtig halten*
work out [wəːk] *ausrechnen*
monetary [ˈmʌnitəri] *finanziell*
indelible pencil [inˈdelibl ˈpensl] *Tintenstift*
boys will be boys [bɔiz, wil] *Jungen sind nun einmal so*
deny *verweigern, -sagen*
you know [nəu] *wissen Sie*
cough [kɔf] *husten*
slightly [ˈslaitli] *schwach, etwas*
jolly [ˈdʒɔli] *famos, herrlich*
chatty [ˈtʃæti] *gesprächig*
on that account [əˈkaunt] *deswegen*
spent [spent] *von* spend [spend] *ver-, zubringen*
beat [biːt] *Runde (e-s Polizisten)*
atrophy [ˈætrəfi] *verkümmern lassen*
powers *Pl* of conversation [ˈpauəz] *Fähigkeiten zur Unterhaltung*
keep the ball rolling [kiːp, bɔːl, ˈrəuliŋ] *das Gespräch in Gang halten*
look after [luk ˈɑːftə] *aufpassen auf, sich kümmern um*
comfort [ˈkʌmfət] *Beruhigung*
go out [gəu] *ausgehen*
live [liv] *wohnen*
pass *vorbeigehen, -kommen*
point to [pɔint] *(mit dem Finger) deuten auf*
face [feis] *gegenüberstehen*
excessive [ikˈsesiv] *übertrieben*
neat [niːt] *ordentlich, gepflegt*
painfully [ˈpeinfuli] *peinlich, übertrieben*
smug [smʌg] *schmuck*

little house of the °double-fronted sort, °lace-curtained, °brass-knockered and °wearing a °lamentable °aspidistra in its lower left-hand window.

'Number Four?' said I. 'That is the home of our Mr. Alaric Thrall. Do you want to be introduced?'

'A friend of yours?' said the policeman.

'No friend of mine,' said I, 'nor of any man, so far as I know.'

'Ah,' said the policeman, and °for a space °considered me °in an absent-minded sort of way. 'I've been °wondering why that window's open, that's all.'

Now that °my attention was drawn to the matter, I °perceived that one of Mr. Thrall's windows was °indubitably open. The window of a room upon the °ground floor, to the right of the neat green door.

'Officer,' I said °admiringly, 'you've an eye like a °hawk. But °it is hardly for us to °question Mr. Thrall's right to open his windows °as and when he chooses.'

'That's °true enough,' said the policeman °mildly. 'But this is a °queer °sort of time to open windows, it seems to me. When I passed °this way twenty minutes ago that window was shut. And why,' said the policeman to nobody in particular, 'a °*downstairs* window?'

I °pondered the matter.

'A sudden °whim, perhaps?' I °suggested °deferentially. 'I shouldn't have thought that Mr. Thrall was °much of a one for fresh air—in fact, this is the first time I've ever seen any of his windows

double-fronted ['dʌblfrʌntid] *mit zwei Vorderfronten*
lace-curtained ['leiskə:tnd] *mit Spitzengardinen*
brass-knockered ['brɑ:snɔkəd] *mit e-m Türklopfer aus Messing*
wear [wɛə] *tragen, hier: haben*
lamentable ['læməntəbl] *erbärmlich, kläglich*
aspidistra [æspi'distrə] *Aspidistra, Schildblume*

for a space [speis] *e-e Zeitlang*
consider [kən'sidə] *eingehend betrachten*
in an absent-minded sort of way ['æbsənt'maindid] *wie geistesabwesend* od. *zerstreut*
wonder ['wʌndə] *sich fragen*
my attention was drawn to [ə'tenʃən, drɔ:n] *von* draw s.o.'s attention to [drɔ:] *j-s Aufmerksamkeit lenken auf*
perceive [pə'si:v] *wahrnehmen, (be)merken*
indubitable [in'dju:bitəbl] *zweifel-, fraglos*
ground floor [graund flɔ:] *Erdgeschoß*
admiring [əd'maiəriŋ] *bewundernd*
hawk [hɔ:k] *Falke*
it is hardly for us ['hɑ:dli] *es ist kaum unsere Sache*
question ['kwestʃən] *anzweifeln*
as and when he chooses ['tʃu:ziz] *wie u. wann es ihm beliebt*
true enough [tru: i'nʌf] *nur zu wahr*
mild *sanft, freundlich*
queer [kwiə] *sonderbar*
sort of *hier: irgendwie*
this way *hier (entlang)*
downstairs window ['daun'stɛəz 'windəu] *unteres Fenster, Parterrefenster*
ponder ['pɔndə] *nachdenken über*
whim [wim] *Laune, Marotte*
suggest [sə'dʒest] *vorschlagen*
deferential [defə'renʃəl] *ehrerbietig, respektvoll*
be much of a one for *hier: viel übrig haben für*

open—but °you never can tell. He is a gentleman of °eccentric °habits, °I understand, and he °keeps odd hours. He lives there alone, you know, and his servants come in every morning. That room is his °study, and if—'

I °became aware that the keen blue eye of the policeman was looking at and through me.

'You seem,' said the policeman, 'to know °a good deal about him. I thought you said he wasn't a friend of yours.'

'I did,' I agreed, 'and that was perfectly true. °Between you and me and my shirt-front, officer, I don't mind saying that if I were asked to °choose between Mr. Thrall and a °one-eyed, °three-legged °mongrel pup with °distemper, °I'd go and buy a °dog-licence at once. But I know him, °none the less. At least, I've met him. °Quite a lot of people have met Mr. Thrall, but he hasn't many friends, I think.'

'Is that so?' said the policeman, in a °far-away voice. And after a little pause: 'Well, that window looks a bit queer to me.'

For another moment he stared at the window as if he °cordially disliked it; then he stepped suddenly from the kerb and went °briskly across the road.

* * *

Nor was I far behind him. Mine is °on the whole a °dull and °uneventful °existence, and I was °in no hurry to °seek my bed. If the open window of Mr. Thrall looked a bit queer to the policeman, it looked no less queer to

you never can tell ['nevə, tel] *man kann nie wissen*
eccentric [ik'sentrik] *exzentrisch, wunderlich, verschroben*
habit ['hæbit] *(An)Gewohnheit*
I understand [ʌndə'stænd] *wie ich höre*
keep odd hours [ɔd 'auəz] *keine festen Zeiten einhalten*
study ['stʌdi] *Arbeitszimmer*
became aware that [bi'keim ə'wɛə] *von* become aware that *merken, daß*
a good deal [gud di:l] *e-e ganze Menge, ziemlich viel*

between you and me and my shirt-front *(eigentlich:)* between you and me and the gate-post (bedpost, lamppost) *unter uns* od. *im Vertrauen (gesagt)*
choose [tʃu:z] *wählen*
one-eyed ['wʌn'aid] *einäugig*
three-legged ['θri:'legd] *dreibeinig*
mongrel pup ['mʌŋgrəl pʌp] *junger Bastardhund*
distemper [dis'tempə] *Staupe*
I'd = I would
dog-licence ['dɔglaisəns] *Erlaubnisschein zum Halten e-s Hundes*
none the less [nʌn, les] *nichtsdestoweniger*
quite a lot of [kwait, lɔt] *ziemlich viel*
far-away ['fɑ:rəwei] *(geistes-) abwesend*
cordially dislike s.th. ['kɔ:djəli dis'laik] *et. gründlich verabscheuen*
brisk [brisk] *rasch u. energisch*
on the whole [həul] *alles in allem*
dull [dʌl] *langweilig, stumpfsinnig*
uneventful ['ʌni'ventful] *ereignislos, ruhig*
existence [ig'zistəns] *Existenz, Dasein, Leben*
be in no hurry ['hʌri] *es nicht eilig haben*
seek [si:k] *aufsuchen*

me, and I was °resolved that the °law should have my company until he °drove me away with °oaths. Life is not so °gay °nowadays that one can °afford to °ignore even the °vaguest promise of °entertainment. Besides, every °Holmes must have his °Watson, and it would be nice, I felt, for the policeman to have me at his side to °gape at his °deductions. So I went after him °at a high speed, and °caught him up as he set his hand on Mr. Thrall's neat little iron gate.

'If it's a °burglar,' I said respectfully, 'I can hold your coat. If °it's two burglars, I can run for help. If °it's °several burglars, I can °take any messages to your °next of kin.'

But the policeman °answered never a word, nor did he °by so much as a glance °acknowledge my presence. Through the gate he went and with a °firm and °purposeful step across the neat little °patch of grass that lay between the house and the road. Arrived at the open window, he stopped, leaned forward across the °sill, pulled aside a curtain and °peered in. I °ranged myself beside him and did °likewise, but the room beyond was dark, and I could make out nothing of any interest.

°'Unpleasant furniture, isn't it?' I said. 'I always think an °antimacassar is a sign of an °ingrowing °mind. I have an aunt who—'

'*Ah!*' said the policeman, so sharply and so suddenly that I jumped. And with that he stepped back a °pace, swung his long legs over the sill and

resolved [ri'zɔlvd] *fest entschlossen*

law [lɔ:] *Gesetz(eshüter)*

drove away [drəuv] *von* drive away [draiv] *vertreiben*

oath [əuθ] *Fluch, Verwünschung*

gay [gei] *lustig*

nowadays ['nauədeiz] *heutzutage*

afford [ə'fɔ:d] *sich leisten* od. *erlauben*

ignore [ig'nɔ:] *ignorieren, nicht beachten*

vaguest ['veigist] *Superlativ von* vague [veig] *vage, unbestimmt*

entertainment [entə'teinmənt] *Unterhaltung*

Holmes, Watson = Sherlock Holmes, Dr. Watson ['ʃə:lɔk həumz, 'wɔtsn] *aus Sir Arthur Conan Doyles Sherlock-Holmes-Geschichten*

gape [geip] *den Mund aufreißen (vor Erstaunen)*

deduction [di'dʌkʃən] *Schlußfolgerung*

at a high speed [hai spi:d] *eiligst*

caught him up [kɔ:t] *von* catch s.o. up [kætʃ] *j-n einholen*

burglar ['bə:glə] *(nächtlicher) Einbrecher*

it's = there are

several ['sevrəl] *mehrere*

take a message to s.o. [teik, 'mesidʒ] *j-m e-e Botschaft ausrichten*

next of kin [nekst, kin] *nächste Verwandte (auch Pl)*

answer never a word ['ɑ:nsə, wə:d] *überhaupt nicht antworten*

(never) by so much as a glance [glɑ:ns] *nicht einmal mit e-m Blick*

acknowledge [ək'nɔlidʒ] *zur Kenntnis nehmen*

firm [fə:m] *fest, sicher*

purposeful ['pə:pəsful] *zielbewußt, entschlossen*

patch of grass [pætʃ, grɑ:s] *Rasenstück*

sill [sil] = window-sill *Fensterbrett*

peer [piə] *spähen*

dropped into the room. All this without a word to me, which °irked me °somewhat; for if my °personality—as some say—is °unimpressive, I like to think that there is at least a something about me that °commands attention. However, it is never my way to °quarrel with policemen, so I said no more about my aunt, but °in my turn threw a leg across the sill and stood within the room.

Of that room which was the study of Mr. Alaric Thrall I have very little to say, and nothing °complimentary. It was just such a room as one would expect the study of Mr. Alaric Thrall to be. A large and airless and °faintly °sinister room, most unhappily °appointed. There was a red °wallpaper that hurt the eye, a red °plush sofa °that was a weariness to see, and four °gilt-framed pictures of the kind that °grocers, there being no law against it, are °apt to °inflict at Christmas upon their more °profitable °customers. Also a leather armchair, a °revolving °bookcase and a °wide desk whereon lay many papers °in confusion. The °atmosphere °suggested that whoever had opened the window had followed no known °precedent.

The policeman was standing by the desk, his back to me; and as I came through the window he °whipped about, saying with °extraordinary °rapidity and °emphasis:

'Stay where you are! Don't touch a thing!'

It was then that, for the first time in my life, I °defied a policeman; for I did

range o.s. beside s.o. [reindʒ, biˈsaid] *sich neben j-n stellen*
likewise [ˈlaikwaiz] *ebenfalls*
unpleasant [ʌnˈpleznt] *widerlich*
antimacassar [ˈæntiməˈkæsə] *Sofaschoner*
ingrowing [ˈingrəuiŋ] *nach innen gewandt, sich abschließend*
mind *Geist*
pace [peis] *Schritt*

---

irk [əːk] *ärgern*
somewhat [ˈsʌmwɔt] *ein bißchen, etwas*
personality [pəːsəˈnæliti] *Person*
unimpressive [ˈʌnimˈpresiv] *keinen Eindruck machend*
command [kəˈmɑːnd] *verdienen*
quarrel [ˈkwɔrəl] *(sich) streiten*
in my turn [təːn] *meinerseits*
complimentary [kɔmpliˈmentəri] *schmeichelhaft*
faintly [ˈfeintli] *schwach, hier: etwas, ein bißchen*
sinister [ˈsinistə] *unheimlich*
appointed [əˈpɔintid] *eingerichtet, ausgestattet*
wallpaper [ˈwɔːlpeipə] *Tapete*
plush sofa [plʌʃ ˈsəufə] *Plüschsofa*
that was a weariness to see [ˈwiərinis, siː] *hier: langweilig aussehend*
gilt-framed [ˈgiltfreimd] *mit Goldrahmen*
grocer [ˈgrəusə] *Lebensmittelhändler*
be apt [æpt] *neigen, hier: pflegen*
inflict upon s.o. [inˈflikt] *j-m aufdrängen*
profitable [ˈprɔfitəbl] *gewinnbringend*
customers *Pl* [ˈkʌstəməz] *Kunden Pl, Kundschaft*
revolving [riˈvɔlviŋ] *drehbar*
bookcase [ˈbukkeis] *Bücherregal*
wide [waid] *groß*
in confusion [kənˈfjuːʒən] *heillos durcheinander*
atmosphere [ˈætməsfiə] *Luft*

not stay where I was. Had I stayed, I could not have seen the thing that lay upon the floor beyond the desk—the thing whose °outflung hand °had caught my eye as I came in over the window-sill. Wishing to see that thing, I defied the policeman and °unobtrusively moved °sideways until I had °achieved my object.

That which lay upon the floor was, or had been, a man; an °elderly man, grey-haired and of a °portly °habit, though tall and strongly °made. He was °clad in pyjamas and a °dressing-gown, and he lay upon his back with his arms thrown out and his head °twisted to one side in an unnatural way. His face was °turned to the ceiling, and it was not a pleasant face to look upon at half past four of a bright June morning. Indeed, it had never been a pleasant face to look upon at any time, so °legibly was °evil °stamped upon its every °feature: the cold, °narrow eyes, the °predatory nose, the thin, cruel, °sneering mouth. This had been an °unloved and °unlovable man, and was now a °very dead man indeed.

Said the policeman, standing by the desk and looking down upon what °remained of this man:

'Your Mr. Thrall—eh?'

'Yes,' I said. 'How—?'

'Broken °neck,' said the policeman, adding °as it were to himself: 'Somebody broke it for him not very long ago.'

At this I °drew a long breath and leant upon the high °back of the leather chair.

suggest *hindeuten* od. *schließen lassen auf*
precedent [ˈpresidənt] *Präzedenzfall, Beispiel*
whip about = whip round [wip] *sich ruckartig umdrehen*
extraordinary [iksˈtrɔːdnri] *ungewöhnlich*
rapidity [rəˈpiditi] *Schnelligkeit*
emphasis [ˈemfəsis] *Nachdruck, Betonung*
defy [diˈfai] *die Stirn bieten, sich widersetzen*

---

outflung [ˈautˈflʌŋ] *ausgebreitet, hier: ausgestreckt*
had caught my eye *von* catch s.o.'s eye *j-s Aufmerksamkeit auf sich lenken*
unobtrusive [ˈʌnəbˈtruːsiv] *unauffällig*
sideways [ˈsaidweiz] *nach der Seite, seitwärts*
achieve one's object [əˈtʃiːv, ˈɔbdʒikt] *sein Ziel erreichen*
elderly [ˈeldəli] *älter(er, e, es)*
portly [ˈpɔːtli] *wohlbeleibt*
habit *Konstitution, körperliche Verfassung*
made [meid] *hier: gebaut*
clad [klæd] *gekleidet*
dressing-gown [ˈdresiŋgaun] *Schlaf-, Morgenrock*
twist [twist] *drehen*
turn *wenden*
legible [ˈledʒəbl] *deutlich*
evil [ˈiːvl] *das Böse*
stamp upon [stæmp] *aufprägen auf*
feature [ˈfiːtʃə] *(Gesichts)Zug*
narrow [ˈnærəu] *schmal, zusammengekniffen*
predatory nose [ˈpredətəri nəuz] *Raubvogelnase*
sneering [ˈsniəriŋ] *höhnisch grinsend*
unloved [ˈʌnˈlʌvd] *ungeliebt*
unlovable [ˈʌnˈlʌvəbl] *nicht liebenswert*
very [ˈveri] *äußerst*
remain [riˈmein] *übrigbleiben*
neck [nek] *Genick*
as it were *sozusagen, gleichsam*

'Then somebody,' I said, °"has done the world a very good turn indeed. There are quite a lot of people who won't weep to hear of this.'

'You think so?' said the policeman.

'That,' said I, nodding at the thing upon the floor, was a bad man, officer, if ever there was one. The °*de mortuis* business doesn't °apply in his °case, because there's nothing good you can say of him, °you see. A real bad man, he was.'

'As bad as that?' said the policeman.

'Worse than that,' said I. 'A °money-lender °by trade and a °blackmailer in his °spare time. °At a guess °I'd say there are at least fifty people °who'd have loved to break his neck and °take the consequences.'

'Well, one of them has done it,' said the policeman, and again he looked at me. 'You seem,' he said, for the second time in ten minutes, 'to know a good deal about him.'

'I do,' said I. 'Because I know a °fellow who once °had dealings with this—gentleman.'

'Ah?' said the policeman.

'The fellow,' I said, °"dropped °a pot of money—°racing—and he came to Mr. Thrall for a °loan. He got it, and he got his °lesson, too. Because when °he'd paid back about twice as much as he'd °originally borrowed, he found there was still a good bit °owing, and he couldn't °raise it anywhere. So he came to Mr. Thrall and asked for a little more time, and Mr. Thrall said he was sorry, but he needed the money at once, and couldn't the fellow

drew a long breath [dru:, lɔŋ, breθ] *von* draw a long breath *tief Atem holen*
back [bæk] *(Rücken)Lehne*

---

has done the world a good turn [dʌn, wə:ld] *von* do s.o. a good turn [du:] *j-m e-n guten Dienst erweisen*
the de mortuis business ['dei 'mɔ:tjuis 'biznis] *das „von den Toten soll man nur Gutes sagen" Zeug*
apply [ə'plai] *zutreffen*
case [keis] *Fall*
you see [si:] *wissen Sie, verstehen Sie*

money-lender ['mʌnilendə] *Geldverleiher*
by trade [treid] *von Beruf*
blackmailer ['blækmeilə] *Erpresser*
spare time [spεə taim] *Freizeit*
at a guess [ges] *bei bloßer Schätzung*
I'd, who'd = I *od.* who would
take the consequences ['kɔnsikwənsiz] *die Folgen tragen*

fellow ['feləu] *Bursche, Mensch*
have dealings with s.o. ['di:liŋz] *mit j-m zu tun haben*

drop *sl.* [drɔp] *verlieren, loswerden*
a pot of money *sl.* [pɔt, 'mʌni] *ein Heidengeld*
racing ['reisiŋ] *(Pferde)Rennsport; Rennen*
loan [ləun] *Darlehen, Kredit*
lesson ['lesn] *Lektion, Lehre, Denkzettel*
he'd = he had
originally [ə'ridʒnəli] *ursprünglich*
be owing ['əuiŋ] *zu zahlen sein, noch offenstehen*
raise [reiz] *beschaffen (Geld)*

—ah—borrow the °necessary from his °firm and—ah—pay it back later? You see the idea?'

'And what happened?' asked the policeman, staring down at the thing at his feet.

But at this point it °occurred to me that we were hardly °exhibiting that °initiative and °resource which the Law expects of those who discover °dead bodies in °the small hours of a bright June morning.

'Don't you think,' I suggested °diffidently, 'we ought to °take steps °of some sort? °What about a doctor, °for one thing?'

The policeman °started and looked °swiftly about the room.

'Telephone?' he °demanded °curtly.

'In the °hall,' said I.

'Stay where you are,' said the policeman as he went out.

* * *

°In the fullness of time there was an °inquest. And at this inquest many interesting °facts °concerning the °late Mr. Thrall were °dragged into the light of day, so that no °single voice was heard to express °regret at his °passing. Indeed, a dead Mr. Thrall was shown to be so °infinitely °preferable to a °live one that the °absence of any °clue °whatsoever to the °identity of his °executioner was generally held to be a °cause for °satisfaction. The policeman (whose name—rather disappointingly, I felt—°proved to be Jones) and I having °severally described our small part in the affair, and such

necessary [ˈnesisəri] *(das) Nötige, notwendige Summe*
firm [fəːm] *Firma, Betrieb*
occur to s.o. [əˈkəː] *j-m einfallen*
exhibit [igˈzibit] *zeigen, entfalten*
initiative [iˈniʃiətiv] *Initiative, Unternehmungsgeist*
resource [riˈsɔːs] *Findigkeit, Wendigkeit*
dead body [ded ˈbɔdi] *Leiche*
the small hours *Pl* [smɔːl] *die frühen Morgenstunden*
diffident [ˈdifidənt] *schüchtern*
take steps [steps] *Schritte unternehmen*
of some sort *hier: irgendwelche*
what about? *wie wär's mit?*
for one thing [θiŋ] *erstens einmal*
start [stɑːt] *zusammenfahren, -zucken*
swift [swift] *schnell, rasch*
demand [diˈmɑːnd] *hier: fragen*
curt [kəːt] *barsch, schroff*
hall [hɔːl] *Flur, Diele*
in the fulness of time [ˈfulnis] *zu gegebener Zeit*
inquest [ˈinkwest] *gerichtliche Verhandlung zur Feststellung der Todesursache (bei ungeklärten Todesfällen)*
fact [fækt] *Tatsache, Faktum*
concerning [kənˈsəːniŋ] *betreffend*
late [leit] *verstorben*
drag [dræg] *zerren*
single [ˈsiŋgl] *einzig*
regret [riˈgret] *Schmerz, Bedauern*
passing [ˈpɑːsiŋ] *Ableben, Hinscheiden*
infinite [ˈinfinit] *unendlich*
preferable to s.o. [ˈprefərəbl] *j-m vorzuziehen*
live [laiv] *lebend(ig)*
absence of [ˈæbsəns] *Fehlen (von)*
clue [kluː] *Spur, Anhaltspunkt*
whatsoever [wɔtsəuˈevə] *hier: welcher Art auch immer*
identity [aiˈdentiti] *Identität*
executioner [eksiˈkjuːʃnə] *Henker*

other °evidence as was available having been given and °debated, the °jury °had no hesitation in °concluding that Mr. Alaric Thrall °had met his death at the hands of some person or persons unknown. The °foreman's manner of °announcing this °decision °implied that, in the jury's opinion, the matter might very well °be left at that. Which—as there was nothing more that could be done—it was.

Now it °came about that some three weeks after the °conclusion of these °proceedings I was bidden to °dine with a Mrs. Wymondham, who lives in Hyde Park Place. This invitation I accepted with °alacrity, for Mrs. Wymondham °happens also to be my °cousin Jane, and what she does not know about the art of giving °dinners has not yet been discovered or °invented. To Hyde Park Place, therefore, I went °on eager feet; and when I had been led to the drawing-room, °endowed with °sherry and °congratulated upon my °association with one of the best °murders of the year, I led my cousin Jane aside and said to her:

'I'm thinking of °starting on my °reminiscences, so show me all the °nibs.'

'I'm afraid,' said my cousin Jane, 'they're a °stuffy °lot to-night—mostly political. Let me see—old Blake you know, and Mrs. Coopington, and Sir Charles and the Wentworth twins. Oh, and there's Mrs. Clinton-Duke —you've not met her, I think.'

'Do you °advise it?' said I.

cause for [kɔːz] *Grund* od. *Anlaß zu*
satisfaction [sætisˈfækʃən] *Zufriedenheit, Genugtuung*
prove to be [pruːv] *sich herausstellen als*
severally [ˈsevrəli] *jeder für sich*

---

evidence having been given [ˈevidəns, ˈgivn] *von* give evidence *e-e Aussage machen*
debate [diˈbeit] *diskutieren, erörtern*
jury [ˈdʒuəri] *(die) Geschworenen*
have no hesitation [heziˈteiʃən] *keinen Augenblick zögern*
conclude [kənˈkluːd] *beschließen, entscheiden*
had met his death [met] *von* meet one's death [miːt] *ums Leben kommen*
foreman [ˈfɔːmən] *Sprecher (der Geschworenen)*
announce [əˈnauns] *verkünden, bekanntmachen*
decision [diˈsiʒən] *Entscheidung, Urteil*
imply [imˈplai] *durchblicken lassen*
be left at that [left] *von* leave it at that *es dabei bewenden lassen*
came about [keim] *von* come about [kʌm] *geschehen*
conclusion [kənˈkluːʒən] *Abschluß, Ende*
proceedings *Pl* [prəˈsiːdiŋz] *Vorgänge, Vorfälle*
dine with [dain] *speisen* od. *dinieren bei*
with alacrity [əˈlækriti] *bereitwillig(st)*
happens to be [ˈhæpənz] *ist zufällig*
cousin [ˈkʌzn] *Kusine*
dinner [ˈdinə] *Essen, Diner*
invent [inˈvent] *erfinden*
on eager feet [ˈiːgə fiːt] *auf ungeduldigen Füßen*
endow [inˈdau] *ausstatten*
sherry [ˈʃeri] *Sherry (südspanischer Wein)*

'Oh, you'll like her,' said my cousin Jane. °'She's a dear and °she's had a very rough time of it. A little while ago she had some awful trouble over money—I don't quite know what—and she was the unhappiest thing on earth. But her son—he's here, too—came home from America and °straightened it out for her, and she's all right again now. Come along.'

°Thereupon she took me by the arm and °conducted me to a far corner, where sat an elderly and white-haired lady whose face bore °unmistakable °traces of that °unhappiness of which my cousin Jane had spoken. But that Mrs. Clinton-Duke was not unhappy now was very °evident from the smile with which she greeted me and the manner in which she turned to the young man who stood—all °cuffs and shirt-front—in the shadow behind her, bidding him come forth and °make my acquaintance.

°Obediently young Mr. Clinton-Duke °emerged from the °background, holding out his hand. I shook it, but in a °dazed and feeble way, for I was °immeasurably astonished. For this Clinton-Duke was a very high, very broad, very efficient-looking young man, with keen blue eyes and very red hair and a chin like the toe of a football boot. So I °goggled at him, and he °frowned at me °ever so slightly, spoke °briefly to his mother and politely but °irresistibly °shepherded me away.

When we were °out of earshot:

°'You'll oblige me,' said he tranquilly, 'by not mentioning that—affair to her.

congratulate s.o. upon s.th. [kən'grætjuleit] *j-m zu et. gratulieren* od. *beglückwünschen*
association [əsəusi'eiʃən] *Verbindung, Beziehung*
murder ['mə:də] *Mord*
start on [stɑ:t] *beginnen mit*
reminiscences *Pl* [remi'nisnsiz] *Lebenserinnerungen, Memoiren*
nibs F [nibz] *großes Tier*
stuffy F ['stʌfi] *spießig, verknöchert, steif*
lot F [lɔt] *Gesellschaft*
advise [əd'vaiz] *empfehlen*

---

she's a dear [diə] *sie ist ein Engel, sie ist so nett*
she has had a very rough time of it [rʌf] *es war ihr sehr schlecht ergangen*
straighten out ['streitn] *in Ordnung bringen*
thereupon ['ðεərə'pɔn] *hierauf*
conduct [kən'dʌkt] *führen, geleiten*
unmistakable ['ʌnmis'teikəbl] *unverkennbar*
trace [treis] *Spur, (An)Zeichen*
unhappiness [ʌn'hæpinis] *Unglück, Elend*
evident ['evidənt] *offensichtlich, hier: deutlich zu sehen*
cuff [kʌf] *Manschette*
make s.o.'s acquaintance [ə'kweintəns] *j-n kennenlernen, mit j-m Bekanntschaft schließen*
obedient [ə'bi:djənt] *gehorsam*
emerge [i'mə:dʒ] *hervorkommen*
background ['bækgraund] *Hintergrund*
dazed [deizd] *betäubt, verwirrt*
immeasurable [i'meʒərəbl] *grenzenlos*
goggle at s.o. ['gɔgl] *j-n anglotzen* od. *anstieren*
frown at s.o. [fraun] *j-n stirnrunzelnd ansehen*
ever so slightly ['evə, 'slaitli] *ganz leicht*
brief [bri:f] *kurz*

She doesn't know I was °mixed up in it—different name, you see—and I don't want her to know.'

'All right,' said I. 'But—'

°'Good show by Kent yesterday,' said Clinton-Duke. °'I'll bet the °bowlers are °cursing this weather. Well, if you'll excuse me, I ought to be—'

'Half a second,' said I. And I °thrust a hand into my pocket and brought out a small, °gleaming °object which I °offered to him upon my °palm. 'This is yours, I think.'

The face of Clinton-Duke became suddenly hard and °blank, and as °empty of all expression as the face of a °wooden °idol. For a long moment he said no word, but stood staring °fixedly at the thing in my hand. A °button it was—a small, shining, °silverish button such as policemen wear down in front of them.

'Where,' said Clinton-Duke, in a very gentle voice, 'did you find that?'

'On the floor under his hand,' said I, 'while you were telephoning in the hall. I kept it because I didn't understand how you came to lose it. But now I think I do.'

'Yes?' said Clinton-Duke.

'I may °be wrong,' I said, 'but this is how it looks to me. °Suppose, now, that I was a policeman and I wanted to °abolish a °bloke who lived on my °beat. I think °I'd °knock him up °on some excuse in the very early hours, °blot him out, leave the window open,. get back on my beat and wait. Then °presently some °innocent °boob would come along, °all flushed with

irresistible [iri'zistəbl] *unwiderstehlich*
shepherd away ['ʃepəd] *fortführen*, F *wegbugsieren*
out of earshot ['iəʃɔt] *außer Hörweite*
you will oblige me ... by not mentioning [ə'blaidʒ, 'menʃniŋ] *seien Sie so freundlich und erwähnen Sie nicht ...*

---

be mixed up in [mikst] *verwickelt sein in*
good show F [ʃəu] *gute Leistung*
I'll (= I will) bet *ich möchte wetten, daß*
bowler ['bəulə] *Bowler (Kricket: der Werfer der Schlagpartei, der auf das gegnerische Tor = Wicket wirft)*
curse [kə:s] *verfluchen, fluchen auf*
thrust [θrʌst] *stecken, schieben*
gleaming ['gli:miŋ] *glänzend*
object ['ɔbdʒikt] *Gegenstand*
offer to ['ɔfə] *hier: hinhalten*
palm [pɑ:m] *Handfläche, hohle Hand*
blank [blæŋk] *ausdruckslos*
empty of ['empti] *bar*
wooden ['wudn] *hölzern; ausdruckslos (Gesicht)*
idol ['aidl] *Götze(nbild)*
fixed [fikst] *unverwandt*
button ['bʌtn] *Knopf*
silverish ['silvəriʃ] = silver(y) *silbrig, silberglänzend*

be wrong [rɔŋ] *sich irren, unrecht haben*
suppose [sə'pəuz] *angenommen*
abolish [ə'bɔliʃ] *vernichten*
bloke *sl.* [bləuk] *Kerl, Bursche*
beat *hier: Revier (e-s Polizisten)*
I'd = I would
knock up [nɔk] *wecken (durch Klopfen), herausklopfen*
on some excuse [iks'kju:z] *unter irgendeinem Vorwand*
blot out [blɔt] *auslöschen, vernichten*
presently ['prezntli] *bald darauf, alsbald*
innocent ['inəsnt] *unschuldig; arglos, einfältig*

wine, and I'd draw his attention to the window and °trot off to °investigate. The boob, naturally, would come along too, and together °we'd discover the body. It would be a kind of °alibi, don't you see? And it would be °dashed °rough luck if I lost a button on my first visit, and the boob °happened to °spot it and wonder how it °got there.'

There followed a little pause, while Clinton-Duke looked at me as if he were seeing me for the first time. And then, quite suddenly:

'You're right,' he said, 'except that I didn't mean to blot him out. He'd been °blackmailing my mother, you see. He had some letters. ... But she didn't tell me till he'd taken her last °cent and was °asking for more. She was °ill with worry, so I °chucked my job in New York and came home. I went to see Thrall, but he °laughed at me and °turned me out. Then I °joined the police, because I had no money, and I had to get work till I'd decided what to do. It was just luck that I was sent to that °division. That morning Thrall came home about an hour before you °showed up. He didn't notice me, and I let him go in. Then I thought it would be a °good chance to °have it out with him, so I knocked him up. I didn't mean to hurt him, but he °turned °nasty and the next thing I knew his neck was broken. Then I took the letters and came away. ... My mother thinks he °repented and sent me the letters before he died.'

'And you're not a policeman now?' I said.

boob [bu:b] *Trottel, Einfaltspinsel*
all flushed with wine [flʌʃt, wain] *voll des süßen Weines*

---

trot off F [trɔt] *ab-, losziehen*
investigate [in'vestigeit] *Nachforschungen anstellen; untersuchen*
we'd = we would
alibi ['ælibai] *Alibi*
dashed F [dæʃt] *verflucht, -flixt*
rough luck [lʌk] *Pech*
happen ... *zufällig* ...
spot [spɔt] *entdecken, erspähen*
got [gɔt] *von* get [get] *kommen*
blackmail ['blækmeil] *erpressen*
cent [sent] *Pfennig, Heller*
ask for [ɑ:sk] *verlangen (nach), fordern*
ill with worry [il, 'wʌri] *krank vor Sorge*
chuck (up) F [tʃʌk] *aufgeben*
laugh at s.o. [lɑ:f] *sich über j-n lustig machen, j-n auslachen*
turn out *hinauswerfen*
join [dʒɔin] *eintreten in, beitreten*
division [di'viʒən] *Bezirk*
show up F [ʃəu] *auftauchen, -kreuzen*
good chance [tʃɑ:ns] *günstige Gelegenheit*
have it out with s.o. *die Sache mit j-m endgültig bereinigen*
turn *werden*
nasty ['nɑ:sti] *gemein, niederträchtig, boshaft*
repent [ri'pent] *bereuen*

'No,' said Clinton-Duke. 'I got a better job a week ago.' He paused again, considering me. 'Well,' he said calmly, 'what are you going to do about it?'

'You remember,' said I, 'my telling you about a fellow I know who borrowed money from Thrall?'

'Ah!' said Clinton-Duke. 'I thought so, somehow.'

'If Thrall hadn't died when he did,' I said, °'the chances are that I'd have done what he suggested—stolen from the firm to pay him back. ... Personally, I don't °think so much of Kent's °batting this year. Anybody could make °runs on the kind of °wickets we've been having lately.'

the chances are that *aller Wahrscheinlichkeit nach*

think much of [θiŋk, mʌtʃ] *viel halten von*

batting [ˈbætiŋ] *Schlagen, Schläge Pl (Kricket)*

run [rʌn] *Lauf (Kricket)*

wicket [ˈwikit] *Wicket, Dreistab, Tor (Kricket)*

The °Fountain °Plays

By Dorothy L. Sayers

'Yes,' said Mr. Spiller, in a °satisfied tone, 'I must say I like a bit of °ornamental water. Gives a °finish to the place.'

'The Versailles °touch,' agreed Ronald Proudfoot.

Mr. Spiller glanced sharply at him, as though °suspecting sarcasm, but his °lean face expressed nothing °whatever. Mr. Spiller was never quite °at his ease in the company of his daughter's °fiancé, though he was proud of the girl's °achievement. With all his (to Mr. Spiller) °unamiable °qualities, Ronald Proudfoot was a perfect gentleman, and Betty was completely °wrapped up in him.

'The only thing °it wants,' continued Mr. Spiller, °"to *my* mind, that is, is °Opening Up. To make a °Vista, so to say. You don't get the °Effect with these bushes on all four sides.'

'Oh, I don't know, Mr. Spiller,' °objected Mrs. Digby in her mild voice. 'Don't you think it makes °rather a °fascinating surprise? You come along the path, never dreaming there's anything behind those °lilacs, and then you °turn the corner and °come suddenly upon it. °I'm sure, when you °brought me down to see it this afternoon, it quite °took my breath away.'

fountain ['fauntin] *Springbrunnen*
play [plei] *in Betrieb sein*
satisfied ['sætisfaid] *zufrieden, befriedigt*
ornamental water [ɔ:nə'mentl 'wɔ:tə] *Ziergewässer*
finish ['finiʃ] *letzter Schliff*
touch [tʌtʃ] *(besondere) Note*
suspect [səs'pekt] *argwöhnen*
lean [li:n] *hager, mager*
whatever [wɔt'evə] *gar nichts*
at one's ease [i:z] *gelöst*
fiancé [fi'ɑ̃:nsei] *Verlobte(r)*
achievement [ə'tʃi:vmənt] *Errungenschaft*
unamiable [ʌn'eimjəbl] *unliebenswürdig*
quality ['kwɔliti] *Eigenschaft*
be wrapped up in [ræpt] *ganz aufgehen in*
. . . it wants [wɔnts] *hier: . . ., was noch fehlt*
to my mind [maind] *m-r Ansicht nach, m-s Erachtens*
opening up ['əupniŋ] *hier: e-e Öffnung zu schaffen*
vista ['vistə] *Ausblick*
effect [i'fekt] *Eindruck, Effekt*
object [əb'dʒekt] *einwenden*
rather ['rɑ:ðə] *vielmehr*
fascinating ['fæsineitiŋ] *bezaubernd*
lilac ['lailək] *Flieder; Pl Fliederbüsche*
turn the corner [tə:n, 'kɔ:nə] *um die Ecke biegen*
come upon [kʌm] *stoßen auf (zufällig)*
I'm sure [ʃuə] *ganz gewiß, hier: denn*
brought down [brɔ:t] *von* bring down [briŋ] *hier: hierher bringen*
took my breath away [tuk, breθ] *von* take s.o.'s breath away [teik] *j-m den Atem verschlagen*

°'There's that, of course,' admitted Mr. Spiller. °It occurred to him not for the first time, that there was something very attractive °about Mrs. Digby's °silvery °personality. She had °distinction, too. A widow and widower of the °sensible time of life, with a bit of money on both sides, might do worse than °settle down °comfortably in a °pleasant house with half an acre of garden and a bit of ornamental water.

'And it's so pretty and °secluded,' went on Mrs. Digby, 'with these °glorious °rhododendrons. Look how pretty they are, all °sprayed with the water—like °fairy °jewels—and the °rustic seat against those dark °cypresses at the back. Really Italian. And the °scent of the lilac is so marvellous!'

Mr. Spiller knew that the cypresses were, °in fact, °yews, but he did not °correct her. A little °ignorance was °becoming in a woman. He glanced from the °cotoneasters at one side of the fountain to the rhododendrons on the other, their °rainbow °flower-trusses °sparkling with °diamond drops.

'I wasn't thinking of °touching the rhododendrons or the cotoneasters,' he said. 'I only thought of cutting through that great hedge of lilac, so as to make a vista from the house. But the ladies must always have the last word, mustn't they—er—Ronald?' (He never could bring out Proudfoot's °Christian name naturally.) 'If you like it as it is, Mrs. Digby, °that settles it. The lilacs shall stay.'

there's that [ðɛəz ðæt] *das stimmt schon*
it occurred to him [əˈkəːd] *es kam ihm der Gedanke*
about [əˈbaut] *an*
silvery [ˈsilvəri] *strahlend, glänzend*
personality [pəːsəˈnæliti] *Person, Persönlichkeit*
distinction [disˈtiŋkʃən] *Vornehmheit, Würde*
sensible [ˈsensəbl] *vernünftig*
settle down [ˈsetl] *sich niederlassen*
comfortable [ˈkʌmfətəbl] *behaglich; sorgenfrei*
pleasant [ˈpleznt] *freundlich*
secluded [siˈkluːdid] *einsam, abgelegen*
glorious [ˈglɔːriəs] *herrlich*
rhododendron [rəudəˈdendrən] *Rhododendron; Pl Rhododendronbüsche*
sprayed [spreid] *besprüht, bespritzt*
fairy [ˈfɛəri] *zart, fein*
jewel [ˈdʒuːəl] *Juwel, Edelstein*
rustic [ˈrʌstik] *einfach, schlicht, roh gearbeitet*
cypress [ˈsaipris] *Zypresse*
scent [sent] *Duft, Geruch*
in fact [fækt] *eigentlich*
yew [juː] *Eibe*
correct [kəˈrekt] *korrigieren, verbessern*
ignorance [ˈignərəns] *Unwissenheit, Unkenntnis*
becoming [biˈkʌmiŋ] *gut stehen*
cotoneaster [kətəuniˈæstə] *Steinmispel*
rainbow [ˈreinbəu] *regenbogenfarbig*
flower-truss [ˈflauətrʌs] *Blütendolde*
sparkle with [ˈspɑːkl] *funkeln vor*
diamond [ˈdaiəmənd] *diamanten, Diamant . . .*
touch [tʌtʃ] *anrühren*
Christian name [ˈkristjən neim] *Vorname*
that settles it *damit ist der Fall erledigt*

'It's too °flattering of you,' said Mrs. Digby, 'but you mustn't think of °altering your plans for me. I haven't any right to °interfere with your beautiful garden.'

'Indeed you have,' said Mr. Spiller. 'I °defer to your °taste °entirely. You °have spoken for the lilacs, and °henceforward they are °sacred.'

'I shall be afraid to °give an opinion on anything, after that,' said Mrs. Digby, shaking her head. 'But whatever you decide to do, I'm sure it will be lovely. It was a marvellous idea to think of putting the fountain there. °It makes all the difference to the garden.'

Mr. Spiller thought she was quite right. And indeed, though the fountain was rather °flattered by the name of 'ornamental water', °consisting as it did of a °marble basin set in the centre of a °pool about four feet °square, it °made a brave show, with its °plume of dancing water, fifteen feet high, °towering over the smaller °shrubs and almost °overtopping the tall lilacs. And its °cooling °splash and °tinkle °soothed the ear on this pleasant day of early summer.

'Costs a bit to °run, doesn't it?' °demanded Mr. Gooch. He had been silent up till now, and Mrs. Digby felt that his remark °betrayed a rather °sordid °outlook on life. Indeed, from the first moment of meeting Mr. Gooch, she had °pronounced him °decidedly °common, and °wondered that he should be °on such intimate terms with her °host.

flattering [ˈflætəriŋ] *schmeichelhaft*
alter [ˈɔːltə] *ändern*
interfere with [intəˈfiə] *sich einmischen in*
defer to [diˈfəː] *sich fügen*
taste [teist] *Geschmack*
entirely [inˈtaiəli] *völlig*
have spoken for [ˈspəukən] *von* speak for [spiːk] *eintreten für*
henceforward [ˈhensˈfɔːwəd] *von nun an*
sacred [ˈseikrid] *heilig*
give an opinion on [giv, əˈpinjən] *e-e Meinung äußern über*
it makes all the difference to . . . [ˈdifrəns] *es gibt dem . . . ein ganz anderes Gesicht*
flattered *geschmeichelt*
consist of [kənˈsist] *bestehen aus*
marble basin [ˈmɑːbl ˈbeisn] *Marmorbecken*
pool [puːl] *Bassin*
square [skwεə] *im Quadrat*
made a brave show [meid, breiv, ʃəu] *von* make a brave show *e-n stattlichen Eindruck machen*
plume of . . . water [pluːm, ˈwɔːtə] *hier: Wasserstrahl*
tower over [ˈtauə] *überragen*
shrub [ʃrʌb] *Strauch, Busch*
overtop [ˈəuvəˈtɔp] *höher sein als, überragen*
cooling [ˈkuːliŋ] *kühlend*
splash [splæʃ] *Plätschern*
tinkle [ˈtiŋkl] *Rauschen*
soothe [suːð] *beruhigen(d wirken auf)*
run [rʌn] *laufen lassen*
demand [diˈmɑːnd] *fragen, wissen wollen*
betray [biˈtrei] *verraten*
sordid [ˈsɔːdid] *niedrig, schäbig*
outlook on life [ˈautluk, laif] *Lebensanschauung*
pronounce [prəˈnauns] *bezeichnen als*
decidedly [diˈsaididli] *zweifellos, offensichtlich*
common [ˈkɔmən] *gewöhnlich*
wonder [ˈwʌndə] *sich wundern*
on intimate terms [ˈintimit təːmz] *auf vertrautem Fuß*
host [həust] *Gastgeber, Hausherr*

'No, no,' replied Mr. Spiller. 'No, it's not °expensive. You see, it uses the same water °over and over again. Most °ingenious. The fountains in Trafalgar Square work on the same °principle, I believe. Of course, I had to pay a bit °to have it put in, but I think it's worth the money.'

'Yes, indeed,' said Mrs. Digby.

'I always said you were a °warm man, Spiller,' said Mr. Gooch, with his °vulgar laugh. 'Wish °I was in your shoes. A °snug spot, that's what I call this place. Snug.'

'I'm not a millionaire,' answered Mr. Spiller, rather shortly. 'But things might be worse in these times. Of course,' he added, more cheerfully, 'one has to be careful. I °turn the fountain off at night, for instance, to °save °leakage and °waste.'

°'I'll swear you do, you damned old °miser,' said Mr. Gooch, °offensively.

Mr. Spiller was °saved replying by the °sounding of a °gong in the distance.

'Ah! there's °dinner,' he announced, with a certain °relief in his tone. The party °wound their way out between the lilacs, and °paced °gently up the long °crazy °pavement, past the °herbaceous borders and the two long beds of °raw little °ticketed roses, to the °glorified °villa which Mr. Spiller had °christened 'The °Pleasaunce'.

It seemed to Mrs. Digby that there was a °slightly °strained °atmosphere about dinner, though Betty, pretty as a picture and very much in love with Ronald Proudfoot, made a perfectly charming little °hostess. The °jarring

expensive [iks'pensiv] *teuer, kostspielig*
over and over again *immer (u. immer) wieder*
ingenious [in'dʒi:njəs] *genial, klug*
principle ['prinsəpl] *Prinzip*
to have it put in [put] *hier: um es anlegen zu lassen*
warm BE [wɔ:m] *wohlhabend*
vulgar ['vʌlgə] *vulgär*
I was *sl.* = I were
snug [snʌg] *behaglich u. geborgen*
turn off *abstellen*
save [seiv] *vermeiden, -hüten*
leakage ['li:kidʒ] *Lecken, Auslaufen*
waste [weist] *Verschwendung*
I'll swear you do *sl.* [swɛə] *und ob du das tust!*
miser ['maizə] *Geizhals*
offensive [ə'fensiv] *beleidigend*
save *ersparen*
sounding ['saundiŋ] *Ertönen*
gong [gɔŋ] *Gong*
dinner ['dinə] *hier: Abendessen*
relief [ri'li:f] *Erleichterung*
wound their way out between... [waund, wei, bi'twi:n] *von* wind one's way out between... *hier: sich zwischen ... hindurchschlängeln*
pace [peis] *schreiten*
gentle ['dʒentl] *hier: langsam*
crazy ['kreizi] *unregelmäßig*
pavement ['peivmənt] *hier: gepflasterter Pfad*
herbaceous border [hə:'beiʃəs 'bɔ:də] *(Stauden) Rabatte*
raw [rɔ:] *ganz neu*
ticketed ['tikitid] *etikettiert*
glorified ['glɔ:rifaid] *gepriesen, gerühmt*
villa ['vilə] *Landhaus, Villa*
christen ['krisn] *taufen*
pleasa(u)nce ['plezəns] *Lustgarten, hier: Lustschloß*
slightly ['slaitli] *leicht, etwas*
strained [streind] *gespannt*
atmosphere ['ætməsfiə] *Atmosphäre, Stimmung*
hostess ['həustis] *Gastgeberin*
jarring note ['dʒɑ:riŋ nəut] *Mißton*

note was °sounded by Mr. Gooch. He ate too noisily, drank far too freely, °got on Proudfoot's nerves and behaved to Mr. Spiller with a kind of °veiled °insolence which was °embarrassing and °disagreeable to listen to. She wondered again where he had come from, and why Mr. Spiller °put up with him. She knew little about him, except that from time to time he °turned up on a visit to 'The Pleasaunce', usually staying there about a month and being, °apparently, well °supplied with °cash. She had an idea that he was some kind of °commission agent, though she could not °recall any °distinct °statement on this point. Mr. Spiller had settled down in the village about three years °previously, and she had always liked him. Though not, in any sense of the word, a °cultivated man, he was kind, generous and °unassuming, and his °devotion to Betty had something very lovable about it. Mr. Gooch had started coming about a year later. Mrs. Digby said to herself that if ever she was in a °position to °lay down the law at 'The Pleasaunce'—and she had begun to think °matters were tending that way—her influence would be directed to °getting rid of Mr. Gooch.

°'How about °a spot of bridge?' °suggested Ronald Proudfoot, when coffee had been served. It was nice, °reflected Mrs. Digby, to have coffee brought in by the °manservant. Masters was really a very °well-trained butler, though he did °combine the °office with that of °chauffeur. One would be comfortable at 'The Pleasaunce'. From

sound [saund] *äußern, hier: kommen*
got on s.o.'s nerves [gɔt, nə:vz] *von* get on s.o.'s nerves [get] *j-m auf die Nerven fallen*
veiled [veild] *verschleiert, versteckt*
insolence [ˈinsələns] *Unverschämtheit*
embarrassing [imˈbærəsiŋ] *peinlich*
disagreeable [disəˈgriəbl] *unangenehm*
put up with s.o. *sich et. von j-m gefallen lassen*
turn up *auftauchen, erscheinen*
apparent [əˈpærənt] *offenbar, -sichtlich*
supplied [səˈplaid] *versorgt*
cash [kæʃ] *(Bar)Geld*
commission agent [kəˈmiʃən ˈeidʒənt] *Provisionsvertreter*
recall [riˈkɔ:l] *sich erinnern an*
distinct [disˈtiŋkt] *klar, deutlich*
statement [ˈsteitmənt] *Angabe*
previously [ˈpri:vjəsli] *zuvor*
cultivated [ˈkʌltiveitid] *kultiviert, gebildet*
unassuming [ˈʌnəˈsju:miŋ] *anspruchslos, bescheiden*
devotion [diˈvəuʃən] *Zuneigung, Liebe*
position [pəˈziʃən] *Lage*
lay down the law [lei, lɔ:] *(alles) bestimmen, den Ton angeben*
matters were tending that way [ˈmætəz, ˈtendiŋ, wei] *hier: daß es dazu kommen würde*
get rid of [rid] *loswerden*
how about ...? *wie steht's* od. *wie wär's mit ...?*
a spot of F [spɔt] *ein bißchen*
suggest [səˈdʒest] *vorschlagen*
reflect [riˈflekt] *überlegen, denken*
manservant [ˈmænsə:vənt] *Diener*
well-trained [ˈwelˈtreind] *gutgeschult*
combine [kəmˈbain] *verbinden*
office [ˈɔfis] *Aufgabe, Funktion*
chauffeur [ˈʃəufə] *Chauffeur*

the dining-room window she could see the °neat °garage °housing the °Wolseley °saloon on the °ground floor, with a room for the chauffeur above it, and °topped off by a handsome °gilded °weather-vane °aglitter in the last °rays of the sun. A good cook, a °smart °parlourmaid and everything done exactly as one could wish—if she were to marry Mr. Spiller she would be able, for the first time in her life, to °afford a °personal maid as well. There would be plenty of room in the house, and of course, when Betty was married—

Betty, she thought, was not °over-pleased that Ronald had suggested bridge. Bridge is not a °game that °lends itself to the expression of °tender feeling, and it would perhaps have looked better if Ronald had °enticed Betty out to sit in the °lilac-scented °dusk under the yew-hedge by the fountain. Mrs. Digby was sometimes afraid that Betty was the more in love of the two. But if Ronald wanted anything he had to have it, of course, and personally, Mrs. Digby °enjoyed nothing better than a quiet °rubber. Besides, the °arrangement had the °advantage that it got rid of Mr. Gooch. 'Don't play bridge,' Mr. Gooch was °wont to say. 'Never had time to learn. We didn't play bridge where I was °brought up.' He °repeated the remark now, and °followed it up with a °contemptuous °snort directed at Mr. Spiller.

'Never too late to begin,' said the latter °pacifically.

'Not °me!' °retorted Mr. Gooch, 'I'm going to °have a turn in the garden.

neat [ni:t] *sauber, gepflegt*
garage [ˈgærɑ:dʒ] *Garage*
house [hauz] *unterbringen, beherbergen*
Wolseley [ˈwulzli] *englische Automarke*
saloon BE [səˈlu:n] *Limousine*
ground floor BE [graund flɔ:] *Erdgeschoß*
topped off [tɔpt] *gekrönt*
gilded [ˈgildid] *vergoldet, golden*
weather-vane [ˈweðəvein] *Wetterfahne*
aglitter [əˈglitə] *glitzernd, strahlend*
ray [rei] *Strahl*
smart [smɑ:t] *adrett; geschickt*
parlourmaid [ˈpɑ:ləmeid] *Haus-, Stubenmädchen*
afford [əˈfɔ:d] *sich leisten*
personal maid [ˈpə:snl] *eigenes Mädchen, Zofe*
over-pleased [ˈəuvəˈpli:zd] *sehr erfreut* od. *glücklich*
game [geim] *(Karten)Spiel*
lend itself to s.th. [lend, itˈself] *sich für et. eignen*
tender [ˈtendə] *zärtlich*
entice [inˈtais] *verleiten*
lilac-scented [ˈlailəkˈsentid] *nach Flieder duftend*
dusk [dʌsk] *Abenddämmerung*
enjoy [inˈdʒɔi] *Vergnügen finden an*
rubber [ˈrʌbə] *Robber (Doppel- od. Dreierpartie im Whist- od. Bridgespiel)*
arrangement [əˈreindʒmənt] *Einrichtung*
advantage [ədˈvɑ:ntidʒ] *Vorteil*
be wont to say [wəunt, sei] *zu sagen pflegen*
brought up *von* bring up *auf-, erziehen*
repeat [riˈpi:t] *wiederholen*
follow up [ˈfɔləu] *(sofort) folgen lassen*
contemptuous [kənˈtemptjuəs] *verächtlich, geringschätzig*
snort [snɔ:t] *Schnauben*
pacific [pəˈsifik] *friedfertig*
me F = I
retort [riˈtɔ:t] *erwidern, entgegnen*

Where's that °fellow Masters? Tell him to °take the whisky and °soda down to the fountain. The °decanter, °mind—one °drink's °no good to °yours truly.' He °plunged a thick hand into the box of °Coronas on the °side-table, took out a handful of cigars and °passed out through the °French window of the library on to the terrace. Mr. Spiller °rang the bell and °gave the order without °comment, and °presently they saw Masters °pad down the long crazy path between the rose-beds and the herbaceous borders, bearing the whisky and soda on a °tray.

The other four played on till 10.30, when, a rubber coming to an end, Mrs. Digby rose and said it was time she went home. Her host °gallantly offered to °accompany her. 'These two young people can °look after themselves for a moment,' he added, with a °conspiratorial smile.

'The young can look after themselves better than the old, °these days.' She laughed a little °shyly, and °raised no objection when Mr. Spiller drew her hand into his arm as they walked °the couple of hundred °yards to her °cottage. She hesitated a moment whether to ask him in, but decided that a °sweet °decorum °suited her °style best. She stretched out a soft, °beringed hand to him over the top of the little white gate. His °pressure °lingered—he would have kissed the hand, so °insidious was the scent of the °red and °white hawthorns in her °trim garden, but before he had °summoned up

have a turn = take a turn *e-n Spaziergang machen*

---

fellow F ['feləu] *Kerl, Bursche*
take *bringen*
soda ['səudə] *Soda(wasser)*
decanter [di'kæntə] *Karaffe*
mind [maind] *wohlgemerkt!*
drink [driŋk] *Drink, Glas*
be no good [gud] *gar keinen Zweck* od. *Sinn haben*
yours truly F [jɔ:z 'tru:li] *meine Wenigkeit*
plunge [plʌndʒ] *tauchen, (ver-) graben*
Coronas [kə'rəunəs] *e-e Zigarrenmarke*
side-table ['saidteibl] *Nebentisch*
pass out [pɑ:s] *hinausgehen*
French window [frentʃ 'windəu] *Terrassen-, Balkontür*
rang the bell [ræŋ, bel] *von* ring the bell [riŋ] *klingeln, läuten*
gave the order [geiv, 'ɔ:də] *von* give the order *hier: die Anweisung geben*
comment ['kɔment] *Kommentar*
presently ['prezntli] *gleich* od. *bald darauf*
pad [pæd] *trotten*
tray [trei] *Tablett*
gallant ['gælənt] *galant, zuvorkommend, ritterlich*
accompany [ə'kʌmpəni] *begleiten*
look after [luk 'ɑ:ftə] *aufpassen auf*
conspiratorial [kənspirə'tɔ:riəl] *verschwörerisch*
these days [ðiːz deiz] *heutzutage*
shy [ʃai] *scheu, schüchtern*
raise an objection [reiz, əb'dʒekʃən] *Einspruch erheben*
the couple of ... F ['kʌpl] *die paar ...*
yard [jɑ:d] *Yard (= 0,914 m)*
cottage ['kɔtidʒ] *(kleines) Landhaus, Häuschen*
sweet [swi:t] *tadellos, einwandfrei*
decorum [di'kɔ:rəm] *Etikette, Anstand*
suit [sju:t] *passen zu*

courage, she had °withdrawn it from his °clasp and was gone.

Mr. Spiller, opening his own front door in an agreeable dream, °encountered Masters.

'Where is everybody, Masters?'

'Mr. Proudfoot °left five or ten minutes since, sir, and Miss Elizabeth has °retired.'

'Oh!' Mr. Spiller was a little °startled. The new generation, he thought sadly, did not °make love like the old. He hoped there was °nothing wrong. Another °irritating thought °presented itself.

'Has Mr. Gooch come in?'

'I could not say, sir. Shall I go and see?'

'No, °never mind.' If Gooch had been °sozzling himself up with whisky since dinner-time, °it was just as well Masters should °keep away from him. °You never knew. Masters was one of these °soft-spoken °beggars, but he might °take advantage. Better not to trust servants, °anyhow.

'You can °cut along to bed. I'll °lock up.'

°'Very good, sir.'

'Oh, °by the way, is the fountain turned off?'

'Yes, sir. I turned it off myself, sir, at half past ten, seeing that you were °engaged, sir.'

'Quite right. Good night, Masters.'

'Good night, sir.'

He heard the man go out by the back and cross the °paved °court to the garage. Thoughtfully he °bolted both entrances, and returned to the library.

style [stail] *(Lebens)Stil; Typ*
beringed [biˈriŋd] *mit Ringen geschmückt*
pressure [ˈpreʃə] *hier: Händedruck*
linger [ˈliŋgə] *verweilen*
insidious [inˈsidiəs] *tückisch, hier: verlockend u. gefährlich*
red hawthorn [red ˈhɔːθɔːn] *Rotdorn*
(white) hawthorn [wait] *Weißdorn*
trim [trim] *schmuck, hübsch, sauber*
summon up courage [ˈsʌmən, ˈkʌridʒ] *s-n Mut zusammennehmen*

---

withdrawn from [wiðˈdrɔːn] *von* withdraw from [wiðˈdrɔː] *zurückziehen aus, entziehen, hier: lösen aus*
clasp [klɑːsp] *Umklammerung*
encounter [inˈkauntə] *begegnen*
left [left] *von* leave [liːv] *fort-, weggehen*
retire [riˈtaiə] *sich zur Ruhe begeben*
startled [ˈstɑːtld] *bestürzt*
make love [lʌv] *den Hof machen, (um)werben*
nothing wrong [ˈnʌθiŋ rɔŋ] *alles in Ordnung*
irritating [ˈiriteitiŋ] *irritierend, lästig, ärgerlich*
present itself [priˈzent] *erscheinen, hier: kommen*
never mind [ˈnevə] *schon gut!*
sozzle o.s. up *sl.* [ˈsɔzl] *sich völlig besaufen*
it was just as well [dʒʌst] *war es schon besser*
keep away [kiːp] *sich fernhalten*
you never knew [njuː] *man konnte nie wissen*
soft-spoken [ˈsɔftspəukən] *gewinnend, freundlich*
beggar F [ˈbegə] *Bursche, Kerl*
take advantage of s.o. *od.* s.th. *j-n* od. *et. ausnutzen*
anyhow [ˈenihau] *jedenfalls, ohnehin*
cut along *sl.* [kʌt əˈlɔŋ] *abhauen*

The whisky decanter was not in its usual place—no doubt it was still with Gooch in the garden—but he mixed himself a small °brandy and soda, and drank it. He supposed he must now °face the °tiresome °business of getting Gooch up to bed. Then, suddenly, he °realized that the °encounter would take place here and not in the garden. Gooch was coming in through the French window. He was drunk, °but not, Mr. Spiller °observed with relief, incapably so.

'Well?' said Gooch.

'Well?' retorted Mr. Spiller.

°'Had a good time with the °accommodating widow, eh? °Enjoyed yourself? Lucky old °hound, aren't you? °Fallen soft °in your old age, eh?'

°'There, that'll do,' said Mr. Spiller.

'Oh, °will it? That's good. That's °rich. That'll do, eh? Think I'm Masters, talking to me like that?' Mr. Gooch gave a °thick °chuckle. 'Well, I'm not Masters, I'm °master here. Get that into your head. I'm master and you °damn well know it.'

'All right,' replied Mr. Spiller °meekly, 'but °buzz off to bed now, °there's a good fellow. It's °getting late and I'm tired.'

'You'll be °tireder before °I've done with you.' Mr. Gooch °thrust both hands into his pockets and stood—a °bulky and °threatening figure—°swaying rather dangerously. 'I'm °short of cash,' he added. 'Had a bad week—°cleaned me out. Time you °stumped up a bit more.'

lock up [lɔk] *ab-, zuschließen, zusperren*
very good *sehr wohl!*
by the way *übrigens*
engaged [inˈgeidʒd] *beschäftigt*
paved [peivd] *gepflastert*
court [kɔːt] *Hof*
bolt [bəult] *verriegeln*

---

brandy [ˈbrændi] *Brandy, Weinbrand*
face [feis] *hier: sich unterziehen*
tiresome [ˈtaiəsəm] *lästig*
business [ˈbiznis] *Pflicht, Aufgabe*
realize [ˈriəlaiz] *erkennen, sich im klaren sein über, begreifen*
encounter *Begegnung, Zusammentreffen, -stoß*
but not incapably so [inˈkeipəbli] *aber nicht so, daß er zu nichts mehr fähig war*
observe [əbˈzəːv] *bemerken, sehen*
have a good time [taim] *sich gut amüsieren*
accommodating [əˈkɔmədeitiŋ] *gefällig, entgegenkommend*
enjoy o.s. *sich gut unterhalten*
hound *sl.* [haund] *Schurke, Hund*
fallen soft [ˈfɔːlən] *von* fall soft [fɔːl] *gefühlvoll werden*
in your old age [əuld eidʒ] *auf deine alten Tage*
there, that'll do [ˈðætl duː] *na, jetzt reicht's aber!*
will it? [wil] *ist das so?, tut es das?*
rich F [ritʃ] *großartig, köstlich*
thick [θik] *heiser*
chuckle [ˈtʃʌkl] *(leises) Lachen*
master [ˈmɑːstə] *Herr*
damn *sl.* = damned [dæm(d)] *verdammt, -flucht*
meek [miːk] *demütig, sanft*
buzz off *sl.* [bʌz] *abschwirren*
there's a good fellow *sei doch so gut!*
get *werden*
tireder *sl.* [ˈtairədə] = more tired
have done with s.o. F [dʌn] *mit j-m fertig sein*

'Nonsense,' said Mr. Spiller, °with some spirit. 'I pay you your °allowance °as we agreed, and let you come and stay here whenever you like, and that's all you get from me.'

'Oh, is it? Getting a bit °above yourself, aren't you, Number °Bleeding 4132?'

°'Hush!' said Mr. Spiller, glancing hastily round as though the furniture had ears and tongues.

'Hush! hush!' repeated Mr. Gooch °mockingly. 'You're in a good position to °dictate terms, aren't you, 4132? Hush! The servants might hear! Betty might hear! Betty's young man might hear. Hah! Betty's young man—°he'd be particularly pleased to know her father was an °escaped °jail-bird, wouldn't he? °Liable at any moment to be °hauled back to °work out his ten years' °hard for °forgery? And when I think,' added Mr. Gooch, 'that a man like me, that was only in for a short °stretch and worked it out °good and proper, is °dependent on the °charity—ha, ha!—of my dear friend 4132, while he's °rolling in wealth—'

'I'm not rolling in wealth, Sam,' said Mr. Spiller, 'and you know °darn well I'm not. But I don't want any trouble. I'll do what I can, if you'll °promise faithfully this time that you won't ask for any more of these big sums, because my °income °won't stand it.'

'Oh, I'll promise that all right,' agreed Mr. Gooch cheerfully. 'You give me five thousand °down—'

Mr. Spiller °uttered a °strangled °exclamation.

thrust [θrʌst] *stecken, schieben*
bulky [ˈbʌlki] *massig*
threatening [ˈθretniŋ] *drohend*
sway [swei] *schwanken, taumeln*
short of cash [ʃɔːt] *knapp bei Kasse*
clean out *sl.* [kliːn] *schröpfen, (aus)plündern*
stump up BE *sl.* [stʌmp] *berappen, blechen*

---

with some spirit [sʌm ˈspirit] *ziemlich energisch*
allowance [əˈlauəns] *(ausgesetzte) Summe, (bestimmter) Betrag*
as we agreed [əˈgriːd] *wie wir vereinbart haben*
above o.s. [əˈbʌv] *hochmütig, stolz, selbstgefällig*
bleeding *sl.* [ˈbliːdiŋ] *verdammt, -flixt*
hush! [hʌʃ] *still!, pst!*
mocking [ˈmɔkiŋ] *spöttisch*
dictate terms [dikˈteit təːmz] *Bedingungen diktieren* od. *auferlegen*
he'd = he would
escaped [isˈkeipt] *entflohen*
jail-bird F [ˈdʒeilbəːd] *Zuchthäusler*
be liable to [ˈlaiəbl] *in Gefahr sein ... zu werden*
haul back [hɔːl] *hier: zurückschleppen*
work out [wəːk] *hier: absitzen*
hard = hard labour [hɑːd ˈleibə] *Zwangsarbeit*
forgery [ˈfɔːdʒəri] *Fälschung*
stretch [stretʃ] *Zeit(raum)*
good and ... *(verstärkend:) sehr*
good and proper F [ˈprɔpə] *schön anständig*
dependent on [diˈpendənt] *abhängig von, angewiesen auf*
charity [ˈtʃæriti] *Mild-, Wohltätigkeit*
be rolling in wealth F = be rolling in money F [ˈrəuliŋ, welθ, ˈmʌni] *im Geld schwimmen*
darn *sl.* [dɑːn] = damn(ed) *verdammt, verflucht*

'Five thousand? How do you suppose I'm to °lay hands on five thousand all at once? Don't be an idiot, Sam. I'll give you a °cheque for five hundred—'

'Five thousand,' °insisted Mr. Gooch, °'or up goes the monkey.'

'But I haven't got it,' °objected Mr. Spiller.

'Then °you'd °bloody well better find it,' °returned Mr. Gooch.

'How do you expect me to find all that?'

°'That's your look-out. You oughtn't to be so damned °extravagant. °Spending good money, that you ought to be giving *me*, on fountains and °stuff. Now, it's no good °kicking, Mr. °Respectable 4132—I'm the man °on top and °you're for it, °my lad, if you don't °look after me °properly. °See?'

Mr. Spiller saw only too clearly. He saw, as he had seen indeed for some time, that his friend Gooch °had him by the short hairs. He °expostulated again °feebly, and Gooch replied with a laugh and an °offensive °reference to Mrs. Digby.

* * *

Mr. Spiller did not realize that he had °struck very hard. He hardly realized that he had struck at all. He thought he had °aimed a blow, and that Gooch had °dodged it and °tripped over the leg of the °occasional table. But he was not very clear in his °mind, except on one point. Gooch was dead.

He had not °fainted; he was not °stunned. He was dead. He must °have caught the °brass curb of the °fender as he fell. There was no blood, but

promise faithfully F ['prɔmis 'feiθfuli] *fest versprechen*
income ['inkʌm] *Einkommen, Einkünfte Pl*
won't stand it [wəunt, stænd] = will not stand it *dürfte dem wohl nicht gewachsen sein*
down [daun] *(in) bar, sofort*
utter ['ʌtə] *ausstoßen*
strangled ['stræŋgld] *unterdrückt*
exclamation [eksklə'meiʃən] *(Auf)Schrei*

---

lay hands on [hændz] *habhaft werden, hier: herbekommen*
cheque BE [tʃek] *Scheck*
insist [in'sist] *beharren*
or up goes the monkey BE *sl.* [gəuz, 'mʌŋki] *oder ich werde fuchtig*
object [əb'dʒekt] *protestieren*
you'd = you should
bloody *sl.* ['blʌdi] *verdammt, -flucht (verstärkend gebraucht)*
return [ri'tə:n] *erwidern*
that's your look-out ['luk'aut] *das ist deine Sache*
extravagant [iks'trævigənt] *verschwenderisch*
spend on [spend] *ausgeben* od. *verbrauchen für*
stuff [stʌf] *Zeug*
kick F [kik] *sich auflehnen* od. *wehren*
respectable [ri'spektəbl] *hier: ehrenwert*
be on top [tɔp] *obenauf sein*
you're for it BE F *hier: du bist dran*
my lad F [læd] *hier: alter Knabe*
look after *sich kümmern um, sorgen für*
proper *richtig*
see? F [si:] *verstehst du?*
have s.o. by the short hairs *sl.* [hεəz] *j-n beherrschen, j-n unter der Fuchtel haben*
expostulate [iks'pɔstjuleit] *protestieren*
feeble ['fi:bl] *schwach, kraftlos*
offensive *anstößig, beleidigend*
reference to ['refrəns] *Anspielung auf*

Mr. Spiller, °exploring the °inert head with °anxious fingers, found a spot above the °temple where the bone °yielded to pressure like a °cracked egg-shell. The noise of the fall had been °thunderous. Kneeling on the library floor, Mr. Spiller waited for the °inevitable cry and footsteps from upstairs.

Nothing happened. He remembered —with difficulty, for his mind seemed to be working slowly and °stiffly— that above the library there was only the long °drawing-room, and over that the °spare room and bath-rooms. No °inhabited bedroom looked out on that side of the house.

A slow, °grinding, °grating noise °startled him. He °whisked round hastily. The °old-fashioned °grandfather clock, °wheezing as the hammer °rose into action, struck eleven. He wiped the sweat from his °forehead, got up and °poured himself out another, and a °stiffer, brandy.

The drink did him good. It seemed to take the °brake off his mind, and the wheels °span °energetically. An °extraordinary °clarity °took the place of his °previous °confusion.

He had °murdered Gooch. He had not exactly °intended to do so, but he had done it. It had not felt like °murder, but there was not the slightest doubt what the police would think about it. And once he was in the hands of the police—Mr. Spiller °shuddered. They would almost certainly want to °take his fingerprints, and would be surprised to recognize a °bunch of old friends.

struck [strʌk] *von* strike [straik] *zuschlagen*
aim a blow (at) [eim, bləu] *e-n Schlag führen (gegen)*
dodge [dɔdʒ] *ausweichen*
trip [trip] *stolpern, straucheln*
occasional table [əˈkeiʒənl] *(Mehrzweck)Tischchen*
mind [maind] *Verstand, Kopf*
faint [feint] *in Ohnmacht fallen*
stunned [stʌnd] *betäubt*
have caught [kɔːt] *von* catch [kætʃ] *stoßen an*
brass curb [brɑːs kəːb] *Messingvorsatz*
fender [ˈfendə] *Kamingitter*

---

explore [iksˈplɔː] *untersuchen*
inert [iˈnəːt] *schlaff*
anxious [ˈæŋkʃəs] *besorgt, bang, ängstlich*
temple [ˈtempl] *Schläfe*
yield [jiːld] *nachgeben*
cracked [krækt] *geplatzt*
thunderous [ˈθʌndərəs] *gewaltig; donnernd*
inevitable [inˈevitəbl] *unvermeidlich*
stiff [stif] *hier: zäh*
drawing-room [ˈdrɔiŋrum] *Salon, Empfangszimmer*
spare room [spεə rum] *Gästezimmer*
inhabited [inˈhæbitid] *bewohnt*
grinding [ˈgraindiŋ] *schleifend*
grating [ˈgreitiŋ] *knirschend*
startle [ˈstɑːtl] *er-, aufschrekken*
whisk round [wisk raund] *hier: herumfahren*
old-fashioned [ˈəuldˈfæʃənd] *altmodisch*
grandfather clock [ˈgrændfɑːðə klɔk] *Standuhr*
wheez [wiːz] *keuchen, schnaufen*
rose into action [rəuz, ˈækʃən] *von* rise into action [raiz] *sich (zum Schlage) heben*
forehead [ˈfɔrid] *Stirn*
pour out [pɔː] *einschenken, -gießen*
stiffer [ˈstifə] *Komparativ von* stiff *stark, scharf*
brake [breik] *Bremse*
span [spæn] *von* spin [spin] *hier: sich drehen*

Masters had heard him say that he would °wait up for Gooch. Masters knew that everybody else had gone to bed. Masters would undoubtedly guess something. But stop!

Could Masters °prove that he himself had gone to bed? Yes, probably he could. Somebody would have heard him cross the court and seen the light °go up over the garage. One could not hope to °throw suspicion on Masters—besides, the man hardly deserved that. But the mere idea had °started Mr. Spiller's °brain on a new and °attractive °line of thought.

What he really wanted was an °alibi. If he could only °confuse the police as to the time at which Gooch had died. If Gooch could be made to seem °alive after he was dead ... somehow ...

°He cast his thoughts back over stories he had read on holiday, °dealing with this very matter. You °dressed up as the dead man and °impersonated him. You telephoned in his name. In the hearing of the butler, you spoke to the dead as though he were alive. You made a °gramophone record of his voice and played it. You hid the body, and thereafter sent a °forged letter from some distant place—

He paused for a moment. Forgery—but he did not want to start that old game over again. And all these things were too °elaborate, or else °impracticable at that time of night.

And then it came to him suddenly that he was a fool. Gooch must not be made to live later, but to die earlier. He should die before 10.30, at the

energetical [enəˈdʒetikəl] *energisch, kräftig*
extraordinary [iksˈtrɔːdnri] *außergewöhnlich*
clarity [ˈklæriti] *Klarheit*
took the place of [pleis] *von* take the place of *an die Stelle treten von*
previous [ˈpriːvjəs] *vorhergehend*
confusion [kənˈfjuːʒən] *Verwirrung*
murder [ˈməːdə] *ermorden; Mord*
intend [inˈtend] *beabsichtigen, vorhaben*
shudder [ˈʃʌdə] *schaudern*
take s.o.'s fingerprints [ˈfiŋgəprints] *j-s Fingerabdrücke nehmen*
bunch [bʌntʃ] *Anzahl*

---

wait up for s.o. [weit] *aufbleiben u. auf j-n warten*
prove [pruːv] *be-, nachweisen*
go up *hier: angehen, aufleuchten*
throw suspicion on [θrəu, səsˈpiʃən] *Verdacht lenken auf*
start [stɑːt] *hier: bringen, veranlassen*
brain [brein] *Verstand*
attractive *ansprechend*
line of thought [lain, θɔːt] *(Denk) Richtung*
alibi [ˈælibai] *Alibi*
confuse [kənˈfjuːz] *verwirren*
alive [əˈlaiv] *(noch) am Leben*
he cast his thoughts back over stories [kɑːst, ˈstɔːriz] *hier: in Gedanken ging er die Geschichten durch*
deal with [diːl] *handeln von, zum Thema haben*
dress up [dres] *verkleiden, hier: sich (so) anziehen*
impersonate [imˈpəːsəneit] *sich ausgeben für*
gramophone record [ˈgræməfəun ˈrekɔːd] *Schallplatte*
forged [fɔːdʒd] *gefälscht*
elaborate [iˈlæbərit] *kompliziert*
impracticable [imˈpræktikəbl] *undurchführbar*

time when Mr. Spiller, under the eyes of three °observers, had been playing bridge.

So far, the idea was °sound and °even, °in its broad outline, °obvious. But now one had to °come down to detail. How could he °establish the time? Was there anything that had happened at 10.30?

He °helped himself to another drink, and then, quite suddenly, as though °lit by a °floodlight, he saw his whole plan, °picked out °vividly complete, with every °join and °angle °clear-cut.

He glanced at his watch; the °hands stood at twenty minutes past eleven. He had the night before him.

He fetched an °electric torch from the °hall and stepped °boldly out of the French window. Close beside it, against the wall of the house, were two °taps, one ending in a °nozzle for the °garden hose, the other °controlling the fountain at the bottom of the garden. This latter he °turned on, and then without °troubling to °muffle his footsteps, followed the °crazy-paved path down to the lilac hedge, and round by the bed of cotoneasters. The sky, despite the beauty of the early evening, had now °turned very dark, and he could scarcely see the tall °column of °pale water above the dark °shrubbery, but he heard its °comforting splash and °ripple, and as he stepped upon the °surrounding grass, he felt the blown °spray upon his face. The °beam of the torch showed him the garden seat beneath the yews, and the tray, as he had expected, standing upon it. The

observer [əbˈzəːvə] *Beobachter*
sound [saund] *vernünftig, brauchbar*
even [ˈiːvən] *einfach, unkompliziert*
in broad outline [brɔːd ˈautlain] *in groben Umrissen*
obvious [ˈɔbviəs] *naheliegend, einleuchtend*
come down to *hier: sich kümmern um*
establish [isˈtæbliʃ] *festsetzen*
help o.s. to [help] *sich bedienen mit, hier: sich einschenken*
lit [lit] *von* light [lait] *beleuchten, erhellen*
floodlight [ˈflʌdlait] *Scheinwerfer-, Flutlicht*
pick out [pik] *herausgreifen, hervorheben*
vividly complete [ˈvividli kəmˈpliːt] *deutlich u. vollständig*
join [dʒɔin] *Verbindungsstelle, Naht*
angle [ˈæŋgl] *Winkel; Aspekt, Seite*
clear-cut [ˈkliəˈkʌt] *klar umrissen*
hand *Zeiger (Uhr)*
(electric) torch BE [iˈlektrik tɔːtʃ] *(Stab)Taschenlampe*
hall [hɔːl] *Diele, Flur*
bold [bəuld] *mutig, beherzt*
tap [tæp] *(Wasser)Hahn*
nozzle [ˈnɔzl] *Mundstück*
garden hose [ˈgɑːdn həuz] *Gartenschlauch*
control [kənˈtrəul] *regulieren*
turn on *aufdrehen*
trouble [ˈtrʌbl] *sich die Mühe machen*
muffle [ˈmʌfl] *dämpfen*
crazy-paved [ˈkreizipeivd] *unregelmäßig gepflastert*
turn *werden*
column of water [ˈkɔləm, ˈwɔːtə] *Wassersäule*
pale [peil] *hier: hell*
shrubbery [ˈʃrʌbəri] *Gebüsch, Strauchwerk*
comforting [ˈkʌmfətiŋ] *tröstlich*
ripple [ˈripl] *Rieseln, Plätschern*
surrounding [səˈraundiŋ] *umgebend*

whisky decanter was about half full. He °emptied the greater part of its °contents into the basin, °wrapping the °neck of the decanter in his handkerchief, so as to leave no fingerprints. Then, returning to the other side of the lilacs, he °satisfied himself that the spray of the fountain was invisible from house or garden.

The next part of the °performance he did not °care about. It was °risky; it might be heard; in fact, he wanted it to be heard if necessary—but it was a °risk. He °licked his dry lips and called the dead man by name:

'Gooch! Gooch!'

No answer, except the splash of the fountain, °sounding to his anxious ear °abnormally loud in the °stillness. He glanced round, almost as though he expected the °corpse to °stalk awfully out upon him from the darkness, its head hanging and its dark mouth dropping open to show the pale °gleam of its °dentures. Then, °pulling himself together, he walked °briskly back up the path and, when he reached the house again, listened. There was no movement, no sound but the °ticking of the clocks. He shut the library door gently. From now on there must be no noise.

There was a pair of °goloshes in the °cloak-room near the °pantry. He put them on and slipped like a shadow through the French window again; then round the house into the °courtyard. He glanced up at the garage; there was no light in the upper °story

spray [sprei] *Gischt, Sprühregen*
beam [bi:m] *(Licht) Strahl*

---

empty ['empti] *ausleeren*
contents *Pl* ['kɔntents] *Inhalt*
wrap [ræp] *einwickeln*
neck [nek] *Hals*

satisfy o.s. ['sætisfai] *sich überzeugen* od. *vergewissern*

performance [pə'fɔ:məns] *Aus-, Durchführung*
care about s.th. [kɛə] *sich et. machen aus*
risky ['riski] *riskant, gewagt*

risk [risk] *Risiko, Wagnis*
lick [lik] *lecken*

sound [saund] *klingen*

abnormal [æb'nɔ:məl] *ungewöhnlich*
stillness ['stilnis] *Stille*
corpse [kɔ:ps] *Leiche*
stalk upon s.o. [stɔ:k] *sich an j-n heranschleichen*

gleam [gli:m] *Schimmer; Glänzen*
denture ['dentʃə] *Gebiß; Pl Zähne*
pull o.s. together [pul, tə'geðə] *sich zusammennehmen*
brisk [brisk] *rasch, flott; energisch*
ticking ['tikiŋ] *Ticken*

goloshes *Pl* = galoshes *Pl* [gə'lɔʃiz] *Überschuhe*
cloak-room ['kləukrum] *Garderobe*
pantry ['pæntri] *Speisekammer*

courtyard ['kɔ:tjɑ:d] *Hof*

story ['stɔ:ri] *Stockwerk*

and he °breathed a sigh of relief, for Masters was °apt sometimes to be °wakeful. °Groping his way to an °outhouse, he °switched the torch on. His wife had been an °invalid for some years before her death, and he had brought her °wheeled chair with him to 'The Pleasaunce', having a °dim, sentimental °reluctance to sell the thing. He was thankful for that, now; thankful, too, that he had °purchased it from a good °maker and that it ran so lightly and silently on its °pneumatic tyres. He found the bicycle pump and °blew the tyres up hard and, °for further precaution, °administered a drop of oil here and there. Then, °with infinite precaution, he °wheeled the chair °round to the library window. How fortunate that he had put down stone °flags and crazy °paving everywhere, so that no °wheel-tracks could show.

The °job of getting the °body through the window and into the chair °took it out of him. Gooch had been a heavy man, and he himself was not °in good training. But it was done at last. °Resisting the °impulse to run, he pushed his burden gently and °steadily along the narrow °strip of paving. He could not see very well, and he was afraid to °flash his torch too often. A °slip off the path into the herbaceous border would be °fatal; he °set his teeth and °kept his °gaze °fixed steadily °ahead of him. He felt as though, if he looked back at the house, he would see the upper windows °thronged with staring white faces. The impulse to

breathe a sigh of relief [bri:ð, sai] *erleichtert aufseufzen*
be apt [æpt] *neigen*
wakeful ['weikful] *schlaflos*
grope one's way [grəup] *sich vorwärtstasten*
outhouse ['authaus] *Nebengebäude*
switch on [switʃ] *anknipsen*
invalid ['invəlid] *Kranke, Gebrechliche*
wheeled chair = wheel chair [wi:l(d) tʃεə] *Rollstuhl*
dim [dim] *verschwommen, schwach*
reluctance [ri'lʌktəns] *Abneigung*
purchase ['pə:tʃəs] *kaufen*
maker ['meikə] *Hersteller*
pneumatic tyres *Pl* [nju:'mætik 'taiəz] *(Luft)Bereifung*
blew up [blu:] *von* blow up [bləu] *aufpumpen*
for further precaution ['fə:ðə pri'kɔ:ʃən] *als weitere Vorsichtsmaßnahme*
administer [əd'ministə] *verabreichen, hier: verteilen*
with infinite precaution ['infinit] *unendlich vorsichtig*
wheel [wi:l] *schieben*
round [raund] *hinüber*
flag [flæg] *(Stein)Platte, Fliese*
paving ['peiviŋ] *Pflaster; Bepflasterung*
wheel-track ['wi:ltræk] *Radspur*
job [dʒɔb] *Arbeit*
body ['bɔdi] *Leiche*
took it out of *von* take it out of *fertigmachen, erschöpfen*
in good training ['treiniŋ] *gut in Form*
resist [ri'zist] *widerstreben*
impulse ['impʌls] *Impuls, Drang*
steady ['stedi] *ruhig, gleichmäßig*
strip [strip] *Streifen*
flash [flæʃ] *aufleuchten lassen*
slip [slip] *Ausgleiten, -rutschen*
fatal ['feitl] *verhängnisvoll*
set one's teeth [set, ti:θ] *die Zähne zusammenbeißen*
kept [kept] *von* keep *halten*
gaze [geiz] *Blick*

turn his head was almost °irresistible, but he °determined that he would not turn it.

°At length he was round the edge of the lilacs and hidden from the house. The sweat was running down his face and the most °ticklish part of his °task was still to do. If he broke his heart in the °effort, he must carry the body over the °plot of lawn. No wheel-°marks or heel marks or °signs of dragging must be left for the police to see. He °braced himself for the effort.

It was done. The corpse of Gooch lay there by the fountain, the °bruise upon the temple carefully °adjusted upon the sharp stone edge of the pool, one hand °dragging in the water, the °limbs °disposed as naturally as possible, to look as though the man had °stumbled and fallen. Over it, from head to foot, the water of the fountains °sprayed, swaying and °bending in the night wind. Mr. Spiller looked upon his work and saw that it was good. The journey back with the °lightened chair was easy. When he had returned the °vehicle to the outhouse and passed for the last time through the library window, he felt as though the burden of years had been °rolled from his back.

His back! He had remembered to °take off his °dinner-jacket while °stooping in the spray of the fountain, and only his shirt was °drenched. That he could °dispose of in the °linen-basket, but the °seat of his trousers gave him some uneasiness. He °mopped

fixed [fikst] *starr gerichtet*
ahead [əˈhed] *nach vorn*
thronged [θrɔŋd] *gedrängt voll*

---

irresistible [iriˈzistəbl] *unwiderstehlich*
determine [diˈtəːmin] *beschließen*
at length [leŋθ] *endlich, schließlich*
ticklish [ˈtikliʃ] *heikel, schwierig, kitz(e)lig*
task [tɑːsk] *Aufgabe*
effort [ˈefət] *Anstrengung*
plot of lawn [plɔt, lɔːn] *Rasenstück*
mark [mɑːk] *Spur, Abdruck*
sign of dragging [sain, ˈdrægiŋ] *hier: Schleifspur*
brace o.s. [breis] *s-e Kräfte zusammennehmen*

bruise [bruːz] *Quetschung, Beule, Prellung*
adjust [əˈdʒʌst] *anpassen, hier: zurechtlegen*
drag [dræg] *schleifen*
limbs *Pl* [limz] *Gliedmaßen*
dispose [disˈpəuz] *anordnen, (zurecht)legen*
stumble [ˈstʌmbl] *stolpern*

spray [sprei] *sprühen*
bend [bend] *sich krümmen* od. *biegen*

lightened [ˈlaitnd] *leichter geworden*

vehicle [ˈviːikl] *Fahrzeug*

roll *wälzen*
take off *ausziehen*
dinner-jacket [ˈdinədʒækit] *Smokingjacke*
stoop [stuːp] *sich bücken*
drenched [drentʃt] *durchnäßt*
dispose of *wegschaffen, beseitigen*
linen-basket [ˈlininbɑːskit] *Wäschekorb*
seat [siːt] *Hosenboden*
mop at o.s. [mɔp] *an sich herumreiben* od. *-wischen*

at himself as best he could with his handkerchief. Then he °made his calculations. If he left the fountain to play for an hour or so it would, he thought, °produce the desired effect. °Controlling his °devouring impatience, he sat down and mixed himself a °final brandy.

made ... calculations [kælkjuˈleiʃənz] *von* make calculations *Berechnungen anstellen*
produce [prəˈdjuːs] *hervorrufen, erzielen*
control *beherrschen*
devouring [diˈvauəriŋ] *verzehrend*
final [ˈfainl] *letzt*

At 1 o'clock he rose, turned off the fountain, shut the library window with no more and no less than the usual noise and force, and went with °firm footsteps up to bed.

firm [fəːm] *fest*

*   *   *

°Inspector Frampton was, to Mr. Spiller's delight, a highly intelligent officer. He °picked up the °clues thrown to him with the °eagerness of a °trained °terrier. The dead man was last seen alive by Masters after dinner—°8.30—°just so. After which, the rest of the party had played bridge together till 10.30. Mr. Spiller had then gone out with Mrs. Digby. Just after he left, Masters had turned off the fountain. Mr. Proudfoot had left at 10.40 and Miss Spiller and the °maids had then retired. Mr. Spiller had come in again at 10.45 or 10.50, and °inquired for Mr. Gooch. After this, Masters had gone across to the garage, leaving Mr. Spiller to lock up. Later on, Mr. Spiller had gone down the garden to look for Mr. Gooch. He had gone no farther than the lilac hedge, and there calling to him and getting no answer, had °concluded that his guest had already come in and gone to bed. The

inspector [inˈspektə] *(Polizei-) Inspektor, (-)Kommissar*
pick up *aufheben, -greifen*
clue [kluː] *Anhaltspunkt, Spur*
eagerness [ˈiːgənis] *Eifer*
trained [treind] *dressiert*
terrier [ˈteriə] *Terrier (Hunderasse)*
8.30 *hier:* p.m. [ˈpiːˈem] (= post meridiem) *nachmittags, abends*
just so [dʒʌst] *ganz recht!*
maid *(Dienst)Mädchen*
inquire for [inˈkwaiə] *fragen nach*
conclude [kənˈkluːd] *schließen, folgern*

housemaid °fancied she had heard him calling Mr. Gooch. She °placed this °episode at about half past eleven—certainly not later. Mr. Spiller had °subsequently °sat up reading in the library till 1 o'clock, when he had shut the window and gone to bed also.

The body, when found by the gardener at 6.30 °a.m., was still wet with the spray from the fountain, which had also °soaked the grass beneath it. Since the fountain had been turned off at 10.30, this meant that Gooch must have lain there for an °appreciable °period before that. °In view of the large °quantity of whisky that he had drunk, it seemed probable that he had had a °heart-attack, or had drunkenly stumbled, and, in falling, had struck his head on the edge of the pool. All these °considerations °fixed the time of death at from 9.30 to 10 o'clock—an opinion with which the doctor, though °declining to °commit himself °within an hour or so, °concurred, and the °coroner °entered a °verdict of accidental death.

* * *

Only the man who has been for years the helpless °victim of °blackmail could fully °enter into Mr. Spiller's feelings. °Compunction played no part in them—the relief was far too great. To °be rid of the daily °irritation of Gooch's presence, of his °insatiable °demands for money, of the °perpetual °menace of his drunken °malice—these °boons were well worth a murder. And, Mr.

fancy ['fænsi] *glauben*
place [pleis] *festlegen*

episode ['episəud] *Episode, Ereignis*
subsequently ['sʌbsikwəntli] *anschließend*
sat up [sæt] *von* sit up [sit] *aufbleiben*

a.m. ['ei'em] (= ante meridiem) *vormittags*
soak [səuk] *durchnässen*
appreciable [ə'pri:ʃəbl] *geraum*
period ['piəriəd] *Zeit(raum)*
in view of [vju:] *angesichts*
quantity ['kwɔntiti] *Menge*
heart-attack ['hɑ:tətæk] *Herzanfall*
consideration [kənsidə'reiʃən] *Überlegung, Erwägung*
fix [fiks] *festsetzen*
decline [di'klain] *ablehnen*
commit o.s. [kə'mit] *sich festlegen*
within an hour or so [wi'ðin, 'auə] *hier: auf die Stunde genau*
concur with [kən'kə:] *übereinstimmen mit, beipflichten*
coroner ['kɔrənə] *Untersuchungsrichter (in Fällen gewaltsamen od. plötzlichen Todes)*
enter ['entə] *protokollieren lassen*
verdict of accidental death ['və:dikt, æksi'dentl deθ] *hier: Urteil, das auf Tod durch Unfall lautete*
victim ['viktim] *Opfer*
blackmail ['blækmeil] *Erpressung*
enter into s.o.'s feelings ['fi:liŋz] *j-s Gefühle verstehen*
compunction [kəm'pʌŋkʃən] *Gewissensbisse Pl, Reue*
be rid of *befreit sein von, los sein*
irritation [iri'teiʃən] *Ärger*
insatiable [in'seiʃjəbl] *unersättlich*
demand for money [di'mɑ:nd] *Geldforderung*
perpetual [pə'petʃuəl] *(be-)ständig*
menace ['menəs] *Bedrohung*

Spiller °insisted to himself, as he sat °musing on the rustic seat by the fountain, it had not really been murder. He determined to °call on Mrs. Digby that afternoon. He could ask her to marry him now without °haunting fear for the future. The scent of the lilac was °intoxicating.

malice ['mælis] *Bosheit*
boon [bu:n] *Segen; Pl Segnungen*

---

insist *beharren, beteuern*
musing ['mju:ziŋ] *in Gedanken versunken, sinnend*
call on s.o. [kɔ:l] *j-n besuchen*
haunting ['hɔ:ntiŋ] *quälend, beklemmend*
intoxicating [in'tɔksikeitiŋ] *berauschend*

* * *

'Excuse me, sir,' said Masters.

Mr. Spiller, °withdrawing his °meditative gaze from the °spouting water, looked °inquiringly at the manservant, who stood in a respectful °attitude beside him.

withdraw from *hier: lösen von*
meditative ['meditətiv] *nachdenklich*
spouting ['spautiŋ] *heraus-, hervorschießend*
inquiring [in'kwaiəriŋ] *fragend*
attitude ['ætitju:d] *Haltung*

'If it is °convenient to you, sir, I should wish to have my bedroom changed. I should wish to sleep °indoors.'

be convenient to s.o. [kən'vi:njənt] *j-m passen*
indoors ['in'dɔ:z] *im Hause*

'Oh?' said Mr. Spiller. 'Why that, Masters?'

'I am °subject to °be a light sleeper, sir, ever since the war, and I find the °creaking of the weather-vane very °disturbing.'

'It °creaks, does it?'

be subject to ['sʌbdʒikt] *neigen zu*
be a light sleeper ['sli:pə] *e-n leichten Schlaf haben*
creaking ['kri:kiŋ] *Quietschen, Knarren*
disturbing [dis'tə:biŋ] *störend*
creak [kri:k] *quietschen, knarren*

'Yes, sir. On the night that Mr. Gooch °sustained his unfortunate accident, sir, the wind °changed at a quarter past eleven. The creaking woke me out of my first sleep, sir, and disturbed me very much.'

sustain [səs'tein] *erleiden*
change [tʃeindʒ] *sich drehen*

A °coldness °gripped Mr. Spiller at the °pit of the stomach. The servant's eyes, in that moment, reminded him °curiously of Gooch. He had never noticed any °resemblance before.

coldness ['kəuldnis] *Kälte*
grip [grip] *ergreifen, packen*
pit of the stomach [pit, 'stʌmək] *Magengrube*
curious ['kjuəriəs] *merkwürdig, seltsam*
resemblance [ri'zembləns] *Ähnlichkeit*

'It's a curious thing, sir, if I may say so, that, with the wind °shifting as it did at 11.15, Mr. Gooch's body should have become sprayed by the fountain. Up till 11.15, the spray was falling on the other side, sir. °The appearance presented was as though the body had been °placed in position °subsequently to 11.15, sir, and the fountain turned on again.'

'Very strange,' said Mr. Spiller. On the other side of the lilac hedge, he heard the voices of Betty and Ronald Proudfoot, °chattering as they paced °to and fro between the herbaceous borders. They seemed to be happy together. The whole house seemed happier, now that Gooch was gone.

'Very strange indeed, sir. I may add that, after hearing the inspector's °observations, °I took the precaution to dry your °dress-trousers in the °linen-cupboard in the bath-room.'

'Oh, yes,' said Mr. Spiller.

'I shall not, of course, mention the °change of wind to the °authorities, sir, and now that the °inquest is over, it is not likely to °occur to anybody, unless their °attention should be drawn to it. I think, sir, all things °being taken into consideration, you might find it °worth your while to °retain me °permanently in your °service at —shall we say double my present °wage °to begin with?'

Mr. Spiller opened his mouth to say, 'Go to Hell,' but his voice °failed him. He bowed his head.

shift [ʃift] *wechseln, sich drehen*

the appearance presented was ... [əˈpiərəns priˈzentid] *hier: es (er)schien so ...*
place in position *in e-e (hier: diese) Lage bringen*
subsequently to *anschließend an, später als*

chatter [ˈtʃætə] *plaudern, plappern*
to and fro [frəu] *hin u. her, auf u. ab*
observation [ɔbzəːˈveiʃən] *Beobachtung*
I took the precaution to dry ... *von* take the precaution ... *hier: habe ich vorsichtshalber ... getrocknet*
dress-trousers *Pl* [ˈdrestrauzəz] *Hose des Abendanzugs*
linen-cupboard [ˈlininkʌbəd] *Wäscheschrank*
change *Drehen*
authorities *Pl* [ɔːˈθɔritiz] *Behörde(n Pl)*
inquest [ˈinkwest] *gerichtliche Verhandlung zur Feststellung der Todesursache (bei ungeklärten Todesfällen)*
occur [əˈkəː] *einfallen, hier: auffallen*
attention ... drawn to [əˈtenʃən, drɔːn] *von* draw s.o.'s attention to [drɔː] *j-s Aufmerksamkeit lenken auf*
being taken into consideration [ˈteikən] *von* take into consideration *in Erwägung* od. *Betracht ziehen*
worth one's while [wəːθ, wail] *der Mühe wert*
retain [riˈtein] *(be)halten*
permanent [ˈpəːmənənt] *ständig*
service [ˈsəːvis] *Dienst*
wage [weidʒ] *(Arbeits)Lohn*
to begin with [biˈgin] *zunächst, für den Anfang*
fail [feil] *versagen*

'I am much °obliged to you, sir,' said Masters, and °withdrew °on silent feet.

Mr. Spiller looked at the fountain, with its tall water °wavering and bending in the wind.

'Ingenious,' he muttered automatically, 'and it really costs nothing to run. It uses the same water over and over again.'

be obliged to [əˈblaidʒd] *verbunden sein*
withdrew [wiðˈdruː] *von* withdraw *sich entfernen*
on silent feet [ˈsailənt] *auf leisen Sohlen*
waver [ˈweivə] *schwanken*

A °Lesson in °Crime

By G. D. H. and M. Cole

Joseph Newton °settled himself comfortably in his corner of a first-class °compartment on the °Cornish Riviera °express. So far, he had the compartment to himself; and if, by strewing °rugs, bags, books and papers about he could make himself look numerous enough to °drive °fellow-travellers away, there was hope he might remain °undisturbed—for the long train was °far from full. Let us take a look at him, and °learn a little about him before his adventures begin—and end.

Age? Forty-five would not be °a bad guess, though, °in fact, he is rather less. °As for his °physical condition, °'well-nourished' is a polite description; and we, who °desire to have no illusions, can safely call him °paunchy, and, without °positive °grossness, °flabby with °good living. His face is °puffy, and whitish under the eyes; his mouth is °loose, and °inclined to °leer.

His fair hair, which is rapidly °growing thin, is °immaculately brushed, and his clothes are °admirably cut and °well-tended, though he has not the art of wearing them well. Altogether he looks a °prosperous, thoroughly self-satisfied, and somewhat °self-indulgent member of the British °middle class; and that is °precisely what he is.

lesson ['lesn] *Unterricht*
crime [kraim] *Verbrechen*
settle o.s. comfortably ['kʌmfətəbli] *es sich bequem machen*
compartment [kəm'pɑːtmənt] *(Wagen) Abteil*
Cornish ['kɔːniʃ] *Cornwall...*
express [iks'pres] *D-Zug, Schnellzug*
rug [rʌg] *Reisedecke*
drive away [draiv] *vertreiben*
fellow-traveller ['feləutrævlə] *Mitreisende*
undisturbed ['ʌndis'təːbd] *ungestört*
far from full [fɑː, ful] *noch lange nicht besetzt* od. *voll*
learn [ləːn] *erfahren*

a bad guess [bæd ges] *schlecht geschätzt* od. *geraten*
in fact [fækt] *tatsächlich*
as for *was ... (an)betrifft*
physical condition ['fizikəl kən'diʃən] *körperliche Verfassung*
well-nourished ['wel'nʌriʃt] *wohlgenährt*
desire [di'zaiə] *wünschen*
paunchy ['pɔːntʃi] *dickbäuchig*
positive ['pɔzətiv] *ausdrücklich, bestimmt*
grossness ['grəusnis] *Grobheit*
flabby ['flæbi] *schlaff*
good living [gud 'liviŋ] *üppiges Leben*
puffy ['pʌfi] *aufgedunsen*
loose [luːs] *lose herabhängend*
be inclined [in'klaind] *dazu neigen*
leer [liə] *hier: schief grinsen*
grow [grəu] *werden*
immaculate [i'mækjulit] *makel-, tadellos*
admirable ['ædmərəbl] *großartig*
well-tended ['wel'tendid] *sehr gepflegt*

His °walk in life? You would °put him down as a business man, possibly a merchant or a middle-sized °employer, not a °professional man. There you would be both right and wrong. He is a professional man, in a sense; and he is certainly °in business.

In fact, he is Joseph Newton, the °best-seller, whose °crime stories and °shockers were °plastered all over the °bookstall he had just left with his burden of newspapers under his arm. He has sold—heaven knows how many million °copies of his stories, and his °serial rights, first, second, and third, cost °fabulous sums to °secure.

But why describe him further? All the world knows him. And now he is on his way to Cornwall, where he has a pleasant little seaside °cottage with twenty-seven bedrooms.

The train starts, and Newton's °carriage still remains empty °save for himself. He °heaves a °fat sigh of relief and °picks up a °magazine, in which he °turns °instinctively to a story by himself. For the moment he cannot remember who wrote it. °Poor stuff, he thinks. He must find out which °'ghost' was °responsible, and °sack him.

Joseph Newton was °interrupted in his °reflections at this point by the °consciousness that someone was looking at him. He glanced up and saw the figure of a man who was standing in the °corridor and staring °fixedly at him, with a °curious °air of abstraction. Newton stared back, trying to look as °unwelcoming as possible. It would be

prosperous [ˈprɔspərəs] *wohlhabend*
self-indulgent [ˈselfinˈdʌldʒənt] *nachgiebig gegen sich selbst*
middle class [ˈmidl klɑːs] *Mittelstand*
precise [priˈsais] *genau*

---

walk in life = walk of life [wɔːk, laif] *Beruf, soziale Schicht*
put s.o. down as [put] *j-n halten für*
employer [imˈplɔiə] *Arbeitgeber*
professional man [prəˈfeʃənl mæn] *Geistesarbeiter*
be in business [ˈbiznis] *geschäftlich tätig sein, ein Geschäft haben*
best-seller [ˈbestselə] *Bestseller-Autor, Erfolgsautor*
crime story [ˈstɔːri] *Kriminalgeschichte*
shocker [ˈʃɔkə] *Schauerroman*
plaster [ˈplɑːstə] *überschütten*
bookstall [ˈbukstɔːl] *Zeitungsstand, -kiosk*
copy [ˈkɔpi] *Exemplar*
serial rights *Pl* [ˈsiəriəl raits] *Copyright e-s Fortsetzungsromans*
fabulous [ˈfæbjuləs] *ungeheuer*
secure [siˈkjuə] *sich beschaffen*
cottage [ˈkɔtidʒ] *Landhaus*
carriage [ˈkæridʒ] *Abteil*
save [seiv] *mit Ausnahme von*
heave a sigh of relief [hiːv, sai, riˈliːf] *e-n Seufzer der Erleichterung ausstoßen*
fat [fæt] *reichlich, hier: groß*
pick up [pik] *in die Hand nehmen*
magazine [mægəˈziːn] *Zeitschrift, Magazin*
turn to [təːn] *sich zuwenden*
instinctive [inˈstiŋktiv] *unwillkürlich*
poor stuff [puə stʌf] *schlechtes Zeug*
ghost = ghost-writer [ˈgəustraitə] *Ghostwriter (Schriftsteller, der für e-n anderen anonym schreibt)*
responsible [risˈpɔnsəbl] *verantwortlich*
sack F [sæk] *'rausschmeißen*

really °bad luck, he felt, if someone were to °invade his compartment now.

The °newcomer, after a moment more of staring, pushed back the door and came in, °flinging down on top of one of Newton's bags a rug and a pillow °done up in a °strap. He seemed to have no other luggage. Newton unwillingly got up and °cleared a corner of his °belongings, and the stranger sat down and began to °unbuckle his strap. Then he settled himself comfortably with the pillow behind his head, and closed his eyes. °'I hope to goodness he doesn't °snore,' Newton thought.

While our second traveller is thus peacefully settling himself for a °doze, we may as well take a good look at him also; for it may be important to know him later on. He is a °scraggy little man, probably of sixty or more, with a completely bald pink head and a °straggling grey beard which °emerges from an °incredibly folded and °puckered yellow chin. His °height is hardly more than five foot six, and his °proportions are °puny; but there is a °wiriness about his °spare person that °contrasts strongly with Newton's °fleshy °bulk.

He is dressed, not so much ill as with a °carelessness °amounting to °eccentricity. His clothes, certainly cut by a good tailor, °hang in bags all over him. His pockets °bulge. His °waistcoat is °buttoned up wrong, and °sets °awry, and his shirt has °come apart at the neck, so that a °disconsolate °shirt-stud is hanging out on one side, while his red tie is leaning towards the other. Moreover, the °sole of one of his boots

interrupt [intə'rʌpt] *unterbrechen, stören*
reflection [ri'flekʃən] *Überlegung*
consciousness ['kɔnʃəsnis] *Bewußtsein*
corridor ['kɔridɔ:] *Gang*
fixedly ['fiksidli] *unverwandt*
curious ['kjuəriəs] *merkwürdig*
air of abstraction [εə, æb'strækʃən] *geistesabwesende Miene*
unwelcoming [ʌn'welkəmiŋ] *wenig einladend*

---

bad luck [lʌk] *Pech*
invade [in'veid] *eindringen in*
newcomer ['nju:kʌmə] *Neuankömmling, Fremde*
fling down [fliŋ] *hinwerfen*
done up in [dʌn] *von* do up in [du:] *zusammenschnüren mit*
strap [stræp] *Riemen*
clear [kliə] *frei machen*
belongings *Pl* [bi'lɔŋiŋz] *Habseligkeiten*
unbuckle ['ʌn'bʌkl] *aufschnallen*
I hope to goodness [həup, 'gudnis] *Gott gebe, daß*
snore [snɔ:] *schnarchen*
doze [dəuz] *leichter Schlummer*
scraggy ['skrægi] *dürr, hager*
straggling ['stræglíŋ] *widerspenstig, unordentlich*
emerge [i'mə:dʒ] *hervorsprießen*
incredible [in'kredəbl] *unglaublich*
puckered ['pʌkəd] *runz(e)lig*
height [hait] *(Körper)Größe*
proportions *Pl* [prə'pɔ:ʃənz] *Ausmaße, Proportionen*
puny ['pju:ni] *klein, winzig*
wiriness ['waiərinis] *Drahtigkeit*
spare [spεə] *mager*
contrast with [kən'trɑ:st] *kontrastieren mit*
fleshy ['fleʃi] *feist*
bulk [bʌlk] *Körperfülle*
carelessness ['kεəlisnis] *Nachlässigkeit*
amount to [ə'maunt] *hinauslaufen auf*
eccentricity [eksen'trisiti] *Verschrobenheit, Exzentrizität*

has °come loose, and °flaps helplessly as his °crossed legs swing slowly to the °rhythm of the train.

Yet, despite these °appearances, the newcomer is certainly a gentleman, and one is inclined to °deem him °eccentric rather than poor. He might be an °exceptionally °absent-minded professor; though, °as a matter of fact, he is not. But who he is Joseph Newton has no idea.

For some time there was silence in the compartment, as The Cornish Riviera °sped °westward past the long °spreading ribbon of London. Newton's fellow-traveller did not snore. His eyes were closed whenever Newton glanced at him; and yet °between whiles the °novelist had still a °queer feeling of being stared at. He told himself it was nonsense, and tried to bury himself in a Wild West story; but the °sensation remained with him. Suddenly, as the train °passed Maidenhead Station, his °companion spoke, in a quiet °positive voice, as of one °used to telling idiots what idiots they were. A °professorial voice, with a °touch of °Scots accent.

°'Talking of murders,' it said, 'you have really no right to be so °careless.'

'Eh?' said Newton, so °startled that his magazine dropped from his hand to the floor. 'Eh, what's that?'

'I said you had no right to be so careless,' °repeated the other.

Newton °retrieved his magazine, and °looked his fellow-traveller °contemptuously up and down. °'I am not aware,' he said, 'that we were talking

hang in bags all over him [hæŋ, bægz] *hier: sind überall ausgebeult*
bulge [bʌldʒ] *sich ausbauchen*
waistcoat [ˈweiskəut] *Weste*
button up [ˈbʌtn] *zuknöpfen*
set [set] *sitzen (Kleidung)*
awry [əˈrai] *schief*
come apart [kʌm əˈpɑːt] *auseinandergehen, aufgehen*
disconsolate [disˈkɔnsəlit] *trostlos*
shirt-stud [ˈʃəːtstʌd] *Hemdenknopf*
sole [səul] *(Schuh)Sohle*

---

come loose *sich lösen*
flap [flæp] *hier: (herunter-) baumeln*
crossed legs [krɔst legz] *übereinandergeschlagene Beine*
rhythm [ˈriðəm] *Rhythmus, Takt*
appearance [əˈpiərəns] *Aussehen; Pl äußerer Schein*
deem [diːm] *halten für*
eccentric [ikˈsentrik] *verschroben, wunderlich, exzentrisch*
exceptionally [ikˈsepʃnəli] *außergewöhnlich*
absent-minded [ˈæbsəntˈmaindid] *zerstreut*
as a matter of fact [ˈmætə] *um die Wahrheit zu sagen*
sped [sped] *von* speed [spiːd] *rasen, (dahin)eilen*
westward [ˈwestwəd] *nach Westen, westwärts*
spreading [ˈprediŋ] *sich ausdehnend*
between whiles [biˈtwiːn wailz] *zwischendurch*
novelist [ˈnɔvəlist] *Romanschriftsteller*
queer [kwiə] *seltsam*
sensation [senˈseiʃən] *Gefühl*
pass [pɑːs] *passieren*
companion [kəmˈpænjən] *Begleiter, Reisegefährte*
positive *bestimmt, selbstbewußt*
used to [juːst] *gewohnt zu*
professorial [prɔfeˈsɔːriəl] *professorenhaft*
touch [tʌtʃ] *Anflug*
Scots [skɔts] *schottisch*
talking of ... [ˈtɔːkiŋ] *da wir gerade von ... sprechen*
careless [ˈkɛəlis] *nachlässig*

of murders, or of anything else °for that matter.'

°'There, you see,' said the other, 'you did hear what I said the first time. What I mean to say is that, if you °expect intelligent people to read your stories, you might at least °trouble to make them °plausible.'

Newton °suppressed the °rejoinder °that rose instantly to his lips. It was that he had far too large a °circulation among fools to °bother about what intelligent people thought. He only said, 'I doubt, sir, if you are °likely to find my conversation any more °satisfactory than my books,' and °resumed his magazine.

'Probably not,' said the stranger. 'I °expect success has °spoiled you. But you had some °brains °to begin with. ... Those °Indian stories of yours—'

Perhaps no other °phrase would have °induced Joseph Newton to °embark upon a conversation with the stranger. But nobody °nowadays ever read or bothered about his Indian stories, though he was °very well aware that they were the best things he had ever done.

'—had °glimmerings of °quality,' the other was saying, 'and you might have °accomplished something had you not °taken to writing for money.'

'Are you aware, sir,' Newton said, 'that you are being °excessively °rude?'

°'Quite,' said the other with calm °satisfaction. 'I always am. It is so good for people. And really, in your last book, you have °exceeded the limit.'

startled ['sta:tld] *überrascht*
repeat [ri'pi:t] *wiederholen*
retrieve [ri'tri:v] *hier: aufheben*
look s.o. up and down [luk] *j-n von oben bis unten mustern*
contemptuous [kən'temptjuəs] *geringschätzig, verächtlich*
I am not aware that [ə'wɛə] *ich wüßte nicht, daß*

---

for that matter *was das betrifft*
there [ðɛə] *da!, na!*
expect [iks'pekt] *erwarten*
trouble ['trʌbl] *sich die Mühe machen*
plausible ['plɔ:zəbl] *glaubhaft*
suppress [sə'pres] *unterdrücken*
rejoinder [ri'dʒɔində] *Erwiderung*
... that rose instantly to his lips [rəuz, 'instəntli, lips] ..., *die ihm unverzüglich auf die Lippen kam*
circulation [sə:kju'leiʃən] *Verbreitung, Absatz*
bother about ['bɔðə] *sich kümmern um*
likely ['laikli] *wahrscheinlich*
satisfactory [sætis'fæktəri] *befriedigend, zufriedenstellend*
resume [ri'zju:m] *wiederaufnehmen*
expect *annehmen, glauben*
spoil [spɔil] *verderben*
brains *Pl* [breinz] *Verstand, Intelligenz*
to begin with [bi'gin] *anfangs*
Indian ['indjən] *indisch*
phrase [freiz] *(kurzer) Satz*
induce [in'dju:s] *veranlassen*
embark upon [im'ba:k] *sich einlassen in*
nowadays ['nauədeiz] *heute*
be (very well) aware that *(sehr wohl) wissen, daß*
glimmering ['glimərin] *Schimmer*
quality ['kwɔliti] *Qualität; Talent, Fähigkeit*
accomplish [ə'kɔmpliʃ] *zustande bringen, erreichen*
taken to ['teikən] *von* take to *anfangen, sich verlegen auf*
excessive [ik'sesiv] *äußerst*
rude [ru:d] *unverschämt*
quite [kwait] *ganz recht!*

'Which of my last books are you talking about?' asked Newton, °hovering between °annoyance and °amusement.

'It is called *The Big Noise*,' said the other, sighing °softly.

'Oh, that,' said Newton.

'Now, in that book,' the stranger went on, 'you call the °heroine Elinor and Gertrude on different pages. You cannot make up your mind whether her name was Robbins with two *b*'s or with one. You have killed the °corpse in one place on Sunday and in another on Monday evening. That corpse was discovered twelve hours after the murder still °wallowing in a °pool of wet blood. The °coroner °committed °no fewer than seventeen °irregularities in °conducting the °inquest; and, finally, you have °introduced three °gangs, a mysterious °Chinaman, an unknown poison that °leaves no °trace, and a °secret society of °international °Jews °high up in the political world.'

The little old man held up his hands °in horror as he ended the °grisly °recital.

'Well,' Newton asked, 'any more?'

°'Alas, yes,' said the other. 'The °volume includes, besides many °misprints, fifteen °glaring °inconsistencies, nine cases of °gross °ignorance, and enough grammatical mistakes to stretch from Paddington to °Penzance.'

This time Newton °laughed outright. 'You seem to °be a very °earnest student of my °writings,' he said.

satisfaction [sætisˈfækʃən] *Zufriedenheit, Genugtuung*
exceed [ikˈsi:d] *überschreiten*

---

hover [ˈhɔvə] *schwanken*
annoyance [əˈnɔiəns] *Verärgerung*
amusement [əˈmju:zmənt] *Belustigung*
soft [sɔft] *leise*
heroine [ˈherəuin] *Heldin*
corpse [kɔ:ps] *Leiche*
wallow [ˈwɔləu] *sich wälzen*
pool of blood [pu:l, blʌd] *Blutlache*
coroner [ˈkɔrənə] *Untersuchungsrichter (in Fällen gewaltsamen od. plötzlichen Todes)*
commit [kəˈmit] *begehen*
no fewer than [ˈfju:ə] *nicht weniger als*
irregularity [iregjuˈlæriti] *Form-, Verfahrensfehler*
conduct [kənˈdʌkt] *leiten*
inquest [ˈinkwest] *gerichtliche Verhandlung zur Feststellung der Todesursache*
introduce [intrəˈdju:s] *einführen*
gang [gæŋ] *(Verbrecher)Bande*
Chinaman [ˈtʃainəmən] *(verächtlich:) Chinese*
leave [li:v] *hinterlassen*
trace [treis] *Spur*
secret society [ˈsi:krit səˈsaiəti] *Geheimbund*
international [intə(:)ˈnæʃənl] *hier: in aller Welt*
Jew [dʒu:] *Jude*
high up [hai] *hier: alles hochgestellte Persönlichkeiten,* F *alles hohe Tiere*
in horror [ˈhɔrə] *entsetzt*
grisly [ˈgrizli] *schauerlich*
recital [riˈsaitl] *Aufzählung*
alas [əˈlæs] *leider!, ach!*
volume [ˈvɔljum] *Band, Buch*
misprint [ˈmisˈprint] *Druckfehler*
glaring [ˈglɛəriŋ] *eklatant, kraß*
inconsistency [inkənˈsistənsi] *Widerspruch, Ungereimtheit*
gross [grəus] *grob, schreiend*
ignorance [ˈignərəns] *Unwissenheit, Unkenntnis*

The stranger picked up the rug from his knees and °folded it °neatly beside him. He °removed the pillow, and laid that down too. He then °moved across to the corner seat °opposite Newton and, taking a °jewelled cigarette-°case from his pocket, °selected a cigarette, °returned the case to his pocket, found a match, °lighted up, and began to smoke. Then he again drew out the case and offered it to Newton. 'Lavery's,' he said. 'I know your °favourite brand.'

As a matter of fact, Newton never smoked Lavery's; but for a °handsome sum he allowed his face, and a °glowing °testimonial to their °virtues, to appear on their °advertisements. Well, he might as well find out what the things were like. He took the °proffered cigarette, and the stranger °obligingly °gave him a light. Newton °puffed. Yes, they were °good stuff—better than might be expected, though rather heavy.

'Now, °in my view,' the stranger was saying, 'the °essence of a really good murder is °simplicity. All your books—all most people's books—have far too much °paraphernalia about them. A really °competent murderer would need no special °appliances, and °practically no °preparations. °Ergo, he would °be in far less danger of leaving any °clues behind him. Why, oh, why, Mr. Newton, do you not write a murder story °on those lines?'

Again Newton laughed. He was °disposed to °humour the old gentleman. 'It wouldn't make such a story,'

Penzance [pen'zæns] *Stadt in Cornwall*
laugh outright [lɑːf aut'rait] *offen herauslachen*
be a student of ... ['stjuːdənt] *... studieren*
earnest ['əːnist] *gewissenhaft*
writing ['raitiŋ] *Werk*

---

fold [fəuld] *zusammenlegen*
neat [niːt] *ordentlich, sauber*
remove [ri'muːv] *entfernen*
move across [muːv ə'krɔs] *hinüberrücken*
opposite ['ɔpəzit] *gegenüber*
jewelled ['dʒuːəld] *mit Juwelen besetzt*
case *Etui*
select [si'lekt] *auswählen*
return [ri'təːn] *wieder zurück-* od. *einstecken*
light (up) [lait] *anzünden*
favourite brand ['feivərit brænd] *Lieblingsmarke*
handsome ['hænsəm] *ansehnlich, beträchtlich*
glowing ['gləuiŋ] *begeistert*
testimonial [testi'məunjəl] *Beurteilung, Gutachten*
virtue ['vəːtjuː] *Vorzug*
advertisement [əd'vəːtismənt] *Anzeige, Inserat*
proffered ['prɔfəd] *angeboten*
obliging [ə'blaidʒiŋ] *zuvorkommend*
gave him a light [geiv, lait] *von* give s.o. a light [giv] *j-m Feuer geben*
puff [pʌf] *paffen*
be good stuff *gut sein*
in my view [vjuː] *in m-n Augen*
essence ['esəns] *(das) Wesentliche*
simplicity [sim'plisiti] *Einfachheit, Schlichtheit*
paraphernalia [pærəfə'neiljə] *Drum u. Dran*
competent ['kɔmpitənt] *tüchtig, sachkundig*
appliance [ə'plaiəns] *(Hilfs-) Mittel*
practical ['præktikəl] *praktisch*
preparation [prepə'reiʃən] *Vorbereitung*
ergo ['əːgəu] *ergo, folglich*
be in danger of ['deindʒə] *Gefahr laufen zu*

he said, 'if the murderer really left no clues.'

'Oh, but there you are wrong,' said the other. 'What is needed is a °perfectly simple murder, followed by a perfectly simple °solution—so simple that only a great °mind could °think of it, by °penetrating to the °utter simplicity of the mind of the murderer.'

'I can't °abide those °psychological detectives,' Newton said. °'You'd better go and read Mr. °Van Dine.' ('Or some of those fellows who would give their ears for a tenth of my °sales,' his expression added.)

°'Dear me, you °quite °misunderstand me. That wasn't what I meant at all. There would be no °psychology in the story I °have in mind. It would be more like °William Blake's °poetry.'

°'Mad, you mean,' said Newton.

°'Crystal sane,' replied the other. 'Perhaps it will help you if I °illustrate my °point. Shall I °outline the sort of murder I have in mind?'

'If you like,' said Newton, who found himself growing suddenly very °sleepy.

°'Very well,' said the stranger. 'Then °I'll just draw down the °blinds.'

He jumped up and °lowered the blinds on the corridor side of the compartment.

'That's better,' he said. 'Now we shall be undisturbed. Now °supposing —only supposing, of course—that there were two men in a railway carriage just like us, and they were °perfect strangers, but one of them did not really °care for the other's face— Are you listening, Mr. Newton?'

clue [klu:] *Anhaltspunkt, Spur*
on those lines [ðəuz lainz] *nach diesen Grundsätzen*
disposed [dis'pəuzd] *geneigt*
humour s.o. ['hju:mə] *j-m s-n Willen lassen; j-n mit Geduld ertragen*

---

perfect ['pə:fikt] *hier: ganz*
solution [sə'lu:ʃən] *(Auf)Lösung*
mind [maind] *Verstand, Geist, Kopf*
think of [θiŋk] *sich denken* od. *vorstellen*
penetrate to ['penitreit] *vordringen bis zu*
utter ['ʌtə] *äußerst, völlig*
abide [ə'baid] *ausstehen*
psychological [saikə'lɔdʒikəl] *psychologisch*
you'd = you should
Van Dine [væn dain] *amerikanischer Kriminalschriftsteller der zwanziger Jahre*
sale [seil] *Ab-, Umsatz*
dear me [diə] *du liebe Zeit!, du meine Güte!*
quite *völlig*
misunderstand ['misʌndə'stænd] *mißverstehen*
psychology [sai'kɔlədʒi] *Psychologie*
have in mind *im Sinn haben*
William Blake ['wiljəm bleik] *englischer Dichter, Maler, Graphiker u. Mystiker (1757 bis 1827)*
poetry ['pəuitri] *Dichtung, Gedichte Pl*
mad [mæd] *verrückt, wahnsinnig*
crystal sane ['kristl sein] *kristallklar u. völlig normal*
illustrate ['iləstreit] *veranschaulichen, erläutern*
point [pɔint] *Ansicht, (Gesichts)Punkt*
outline ['autlain] *skizzieren, in groben Zügen darstellen*
sleepy ['sli:pi] *schläfrig, müde*
very well *nun gut*
I'll = I will
blind [blaind] *Jalousie, Rouleau*
lower ['ləuə] *herunterlassen*
supposing [sə'pəuziŋ] *angenommen*

'Yes,' said Newton, very sleepily. He was now having real difficulty in keeping his eyes open.

'And, °further, supposing neither of them had brought any special °paraphernalia with him, except what any °innocent traveller might be carrying—say, a rug, a pillow, and a rug-strap—'

As he spoke, the stranger picked up the rug-strap from the seat beside him.

'Hey, what's that about a rug-strap?' said Newton °roused for a moment by a °connection of ideas he was too sleepy to °sort out.

'Except, of course, just one °doped cigarette, containing an °opiate—strong, but in no wise °fatal,' the other went on °blandly.

°'What the—?' murmured Newton, °struggling now °vainly against an °absolutely °stupefying °drowsiness.

'There would really be nothing to °prevent him from committing a nice, neat murder, would there?' the old man continued, rising as he spoke with °startling °agility and °flinging the °loop of the rug-strap over Newton's head. 'Now would there?' he repeated, as he drew it °tight around his °victim's neck and neatly °fastened it. Newton's mouth came wide open; his tongue °protruded, and he began to °gurgle °horribly; his eyes °stuck out from his head.

'And then,' said the stranger, 'the pillow would °come in so handy to °finish him off.' He °dragged Newton down on the seat, °placed the pillow °firmly on his °upturned face, and sat

perfect strangers *Pl* [ˈstreindʒəz] *wildfremde Leute*
care for [kɛə] *(gern) mögen*

---

further [ˈfəːðə] *überdies*
paraphernalia *hier: Ausrüstung, Tatwerkzeug*
innocent [ˈinəsnt] *harmlos*
rouse [rauz] *wachrütteln*
connection of ideas [kəˈnekʃən, aiˈdiəz] *Gedankenverbindung*
sort out [sɔːt] *sortieren, einordnen*
doped [dəupt] *hier: präpariert*
opiate [ˈəupiit] *Opiat, Schlafmittel*
fatal [ˈfeitl] *tödlich*
bland [blænd] *gelassen, kühl*
what the ... *was zum ...*
struggle against [ˈstrʌgl] *ankämpfen gegen*
vain [vein] *vergeblich*
absolutely [ˈæbsəluːtli] *vollkommen, völlig*
stupefying [ˈstjuːpifaiiŋ] *betäubend*
drowsiness [ˈdrauzinis] *Schläfrigkeit*
prevent from [priˈvent] *hindern an*
startling [ˈstɑːtliŋ] *überraschend*
agility [əˈdʒiliti] *Beweglichkeit, Behendigkeit*
fling *werfen, schleudern*
loop [luːp] *Schlinge*
tight [tait] *fest*
victim [ˈviktim] *Opfer*
fasten [ˈfɑːsn] *befestigen*
protrude [prəˈtruːd] *heraustreten*
gurgle [ˈgəːgl] *gurgeln*
horrible [ˈhɔrəbl] *fürchterlich, grauenvoll*
stuck out [stʌk] *von* stick out [stik] *hervorstehen, hier: herausquellen*
come in handy [kʌm, ˈhændi] *gelegen kommen*
finish s.o. off F [ˈfiniʃ] *j-n erledigen*
drag [dræg] *zerren, ziehen*
place [pleis] *legen, hier: drücken*
firm [fəːm] *fest*
upturned [ˈʌpˈtəːnd] *nach oben gekehrt*

on it, smiling °delightedly. The °gurgling slowly °ceased.

'The rug,' the °cheerful voice went on, 'has °proved to be °superfluous. Really, Mr. Newton, murder is even easier than I supposed—though it is not often, I °imagine, that a °lucky chance °enables one to °do a service to the °literary °craft at the same time.'

Newton said nothing; for he was dead.

The stranger °retained his °position a little longer, still smiling gently to himself. Then he rose, removed the pillow from Newton's face, and, after a careful °survey of the °body, °undid the strap. Next, he °picked up a half-smoked cigarette and threw it out of the window, folded his rug neatly, °did it and the pillow up in the strap, and, opening the door into the corridor, walked quietly away °down the train.

°'What a pity!' he murmured to himself as he went. 'It would make such a good story; and I am afraid the poor fellow will never °have the sense to write it.'

The body of Joseph Newton was °actually discovered by a °restaurant-car °attendant who was going round to °collect °orders for the first lunch. Opening the door of a first-class compartment, which had all its blinds drawn down, he found Newton, no °pleasant °sight and °indubitably dead, stretched out upon the seat where his companion had left him.

°Without waiting to do more than °make sure the man was dead, he

delighted [di'laitid] *vergnügt, entzückt*
gurgling ['gəːgliŋ] *Gurgeln*
cease [siːs] *aufhören*
cheerful ['tʃiəful] *fröhlich, vergnügt*
prove (to be) [pruːv] *sich herausstellen* od. *erweisen als*
superfluous [sju(ː)'pəːfluəs] *überflüssig*
imagine [i'mædʒin] *glauben*
lucky chance ['lʌki tʃɑːns] *glücklicher Zufall*
enable s.o. [i'neibl] *es j-m ermöglichen*
do a service to s.o. ['səːvis] *j-m e-n Dienst erweisen*
literary ['litərəri] *literarisch*
craft [krɑːft] *Zunft; Handwerk*
retain [ri'tein] *beibehalten*
position [pə'ziʃən] *Stellung, Lage*
survey ['səːvei] *Inspektion, Prüfung*
body ['bɔdi] *Leiche*
undid ['ʌn'did] *von* undo ['ʌn'duː] *lösen, aufknüpfen*
pick up *aufheben*
did up *von* do up *ver-, zusammenschnüren*
down the train [daun, trein] *im Zug nach hinten*
what a pity ['piti] *wie schade!*
have the sense to do s.th. [sens] *so klug sein, et. zu tun*
actually ['æktʃuəli] *in der Tat*
restaurant car ['restərɔ̃ːŋ, 'restərɔnt, kɑː] *Speisewagen*
attendant [ə'tendənt] *Bedienstete, Angestellte*
collect [kə'lekt] *hier: entgegennehmen*
order ['ɔːdə] *Bestellung*
pleasant *erfreulich*
sight [sait] *Anblick*
indubitable [in'djuːbitəbl] *unzweifelhaft, fraglos*
without waiting to do more than ... [wi'ðaut, 'weitiŋ, mɔː] *hier: ohne länger zu bleiben als nötig war, um zu ...*
make sure [ʃuə] *sich (davon) überzeugen, daß*

°scuttled along to fetch the °guard. A °brief °colloquy of °train-officials then took place in the °fatal compartment, and it was °decided to stop the train °short of Newbury Station, and °send for the police before anyone had a °chance of leaving it. It seemed clear, as there had been no stop since they left Paddington, that the murderer must still °be on it, unless he had leaped from an express °travelling °at full speed.

The police °duly arrived, °inspected the body, °hunted the compartment in vain for traces of another passenger—for the murderer °had taken the precaution of wearing gloves °throughout his °demonstration—°took the name and address of every person on the train, °to the number of some hundreds, had the carriage in which the murder had °occurred °detached, with much °shunting and °grunting, from the rest of the train, and finally allowed the °delayed express to °proceed.

Only those travellers who had been actually in the °coach of which Newton's compartment had formed a part were kept back for further °inquiries. But Newton's companion was not among them. Having given his correct name and address to the police, he °proceeded quietly upon his journey in the empty first-class compartment two coaches farther back to which he had moved after his successful °experiment in simplicity.

There were four hundred and ninety-eight passengers on the Cornish Riviera

scuttle along [ˈskʌtl əˈlɔŋ] *weiter-, forteilen*
guard [gɑːd] *Zugführer; Schaffner*
brief [briːf] *kurz*
colloquy [ˈkɔləkwi] *Unterhaltung, Gespräch*
train-official [ˈtreinəˈfiʃəl] *Zugbeamte*
fatal *Todes...*
decide [diˈsaid] *beschließen*
short of [ʃɔːt] *(kurz) vor*
send for [send] *holen (lassen)*
chance [tʃɑːns] *Gelegenheit, Möglichkeit*
be on it *hier: im Zug sein*
travel [ˈtrævl] *dahinrasen*
at full speed [ful spiːd] *mit höchster Geschwindigkeit*
duly [ˈdjuːli] *pünktlich*
inspect [inˈspekt] *sich genau ansehen*
hunt for [hʌnt] *ab-* od. *durchsuchen nach*
had taken the precaution [priˈkɔːʃən] *von* take the precaution *die Vorsichtsmaßnahme treffen*
throughout [θru(ː)ˈaut] *während*
demonstration [demənˈstreiʃən] *Demonstration, Vorführung*
took [tuk] *von* take *sich notieren* od. *aufschreiben*
to the number of some ... [ˈnʌmbə, sʌm] *einige ... an der Zahl*
occur [əˈkəː] *sich ereignen, geschehen*
detach [diˈtætʃ] *hier: abkoppeln*
shunting [ˈʃʌntiŋ] *Rangieren*
grunting [ˈgrʌntiŋ] *Murren*
delayed [diˈleid] *verspätet*
proceed [prəˈsiːd] *hier: s-e Reise fortsetzen*
coach [kəutʃ] *Waggon, Wagen*
inquiry [inˈkwaiəri] *Ermittlung, Nachforschung, Frage*
proceed upon one's journey [ˈdʒəːni] *weiterreisen, s-e Reise fortsetzen*
experiment in simplicity [iksˈperimənt] *Experiment auf dem Gebiet der Einfachheit*

express whose names were taken by the police at Newbury; or, if you count Newton, four hundred and ninety-nine. Add guards and attendants, restaurant-car °staff, and the °occupants of a °travelling °Post Office van—°total five hundred and nineteen.

Of these one hundred and twenty-six were women, one hundred and fifty-three children, and the rest men. That °allowed for quite enough possible °suspects for the police to °follow up. They were followed up, °exhaustively. But it did not °appear that any single person among them °had any acquaintance with Joseph Newton, or any connection with him save as readers of his books. Nor did a °meticulous examination of Newton's °past °suggest the °shadow of a reason why he should have been murdered.

The police °tried their hardest, and °the public and °the Press did their best to assist, for the murder of a best-seller, by a criminal who left no clue, was enough to °excite anybody's °imagination. Several °individuals, in their enthusiasm, went so far as to °confess to the crime, and gave Scotland Yard several days' work in °disproving their °statements. But nothing helpful was °forthcoming, and °at long last the °excitement °died down.

It was more than three months later that the young Marquis of Queensferry °called upon Henry Wilson, °formerly the °chief °official of Scotland Yard, and now the °foremost °private detective in England. His °mod-

staff [stɑːf] *Personal*
occupant [ˈɔkjupənt] *Insasse*
travelling [ˈtrævliŋ] *fahrbar, auf Rädern*
post office van [pəust ˈɔfis væn] *Postwagen*
total [ˈtəutl] *gesamt; insgesamt sein*
allow for [əˈlau] *hier: (übrig-) lassen*
suspect [ˈsʌspekt] *Verdächtige*
follow up [ˈfɔləu] *hier: weitere Nachforschungen (über sie) anstellen*
exhaustive [igˈzɔːstiv] *erschöpfend, ganz gründlich*
appear [əˈpiə] *aussehen*
have any acquaintance with [əˈkweintəns] *irgendwie bekannt sein mit*
meticulous [miˈtikjuləs] *peinlich genau*
past [pɑːst] *Vergangenheit*
suggest [səˈdʒest] *schließen lassen auf*
shadow of a reason [ˈʃædəu, ˈriːzn] *geringste Grund*
try one's hardest [trai, ˈhɑːdist] *sich alle Mühe geben*
the public [ˈpʌblik] *die Öffentlichkeit*
the press [pres] *die Presse*
excite [ikˈsait] *erregen, hier: anregen*
imagination [imædʒiˈneiʃən] *Phantasie, Einbildungskraft*
individual [indiˈvidjuəl] *Person*
confess to [kənˈfes] *gestehen*
disprove [ˈdisˈpruːv] *widerlegen*
statement [ˈsteitmənt] *Aussage*
be forthcoming [fɔːθˈkʌmiŋ] *zum Vorschein kommen*
at long last [lɑːst] *schließlich*
excitement [ikˈsaitmənt] *Aufregung*
die down [dai] *sich legen*
call upon s.o. [kɔːl] *e-n Besuch machen bei j-m*
formerly [ˈfɔːməli] *ehemals*
chief [tʃiːf] *höchst(er, e, es)*
official [əˈfiʃəl] *Beamte*
foremost [ˈfɔːməust] *erst(er, e, es)*
private detective [ˈpraivit] *Privatdetektiv*
modest [ˈmɔdist] *bescheiden*

est °request was that Wilson should °solve for him the °mystery of Joseph Newton's murder.

When Wilson asked him why he wanted it solved, the Marquis explained that it was for a °bet. It °appeared that his old uncle, the °Honourable Roderick Dominic °Acres-Noel, had °bet him fifty thousand pounds °to a penny he could not solve the °problem, and he, who had the °title but not the money, would °be very willing to °lay his hands on fifty thousand pounds which his uncle, who had the money but not the title, would never °miss. Asked the reason for so unusual a bet, he replied that the reason was Uncle Roderick, who was always betting on something, °the sillier the better.

'Our family's like that, °you know,' the Marquis added. 'We're all mad. And my uncle was quite °excited about the case, because he was on the train when it happened. He even wrote to *The Times* about it.'

Wilson °rejected the idea that he could solve a case which had °utterly °baffled Scotland Yard when the °trail was fresh, now that it was °stone cold, and all clues, °presumably, °vanished into limbo. Even the most °lavish promises of °shares in the fifty thousand pounds did not °tempt him, and he °sent the young Marquis away with a flea in his ear.

But, after the Marquis had gone, he found that he could not get the case out of his head. °In common with everybody else, he had °puzzled his brains

request [ri'kwest] *Bitte, Wunsch*
solve [sɔlv] *lösen, aufklären*
mystery ['mistəri] *Geheimnis, Rätsel*
bet [bet] *Wette*
appear *sich herausstellen*
Honourable ['ɔnərəbl] *(der, die) Ehrenwerte*
Acres-Noel ['eikəz'nəuəl] *Familienname*
bet s.o. ... *mit j-m wetten um ...*
to a penny ['peni] *auf den Penny* od. *Pfennig genau*
problem ['prɔbləm] *Rätsel*
title ['taitl] *(Adels)Titel*
be willing to do s.th. ['wiliŋ] *gern et. tun*
lay one's hands on [lei, hændz] *in die Hand bekommen, habhaft werden*
miss [mis] *vermissen*
the ... the *je ... desto*
you know [nəu] *wissen Sie*
excited [ik'saitid] *aufgeregt*
reject [ri'dʒekt] *zurückweisen*
utterly ['ʌtəli] *völlig*
baffle ['bæfl] *verwirren, (j-m) ein Rätsel sein*
trail [treil] *Spur, Fährte*
stone cold [stəun kəuld] *eiskalt*
presumable [pri'zju:məbl] *vermutlich*
vanish into limbo ['væniʃ, 'limbəu] *hier: sich in Nichts auflösen*
lavish ['læviʃ] *verschwenderisch*
share [ʃɛə] *Anteil*
tempt [tempt] *in Versuchung führen*
sent s.o. away with a flea in his ear [sent, fli:, iə] *von* send s.o. away ... [send] *j-n abweisen,* F *j-n abfahren lassen*
in common with ['kɔmən] *(genau) wie*
puzzle one's brains ['pʌzl] *sich den Kopf zerbrechen*

over it at the time; but it was weeks since he °had given it a thought. But now—here it was again—°bothering his mind.

°Hang it all, it wasn't °reasonable—it was against nature—that a man should be able to murder another man and °get away without leaving any clue at all. So, °at any rate, the Marquis's crazy old uncle seemed to think, unless, indeed, he was °merely crazy. °Most likely he was.

Wilson could not say exactly at what moment he °decided to °have one more shot at this impossible mystery. Perhaps it was when he °recollected that, °according to the Marquis, Mr. Acres-Noel had himself °travelled on that train to Cornwall. It might be that Mr. Acres-Noel had °noticed something that the police had °missed; he was just the sort of old gentleman who would °enjoy °keeping a °titbit of information to himself. At any rate, it was one thing one could try.

Wilson °rang up his old °colleague, °Inspector Blaikie, at Scotland Yard, and Blaikie °guffawed at him.

'Solve it, °by all means,' he said. 'We'll °be delighted. °We're sick of the sound of Newton's name. ... Yes, old Acres-Noel was on the train—I don't know anything more about him. ... Oh, °mad as a hatter. °Completely. ... Yes, he wrote to *The Times*, and they °printed it. ... Three days afterwards, I think. Shall I °have it looked up for you? ... °Right you are. Let us know when you catch the murderer, won't you?'

had given it a thought [ˈgivn, θɔːt] *von* give thought to *sich Gedanken machen über*
bother *plagen, beunruhigen, nicht in Ruhe lassen*
hang it (all) F [hæŋ] *zum Henker damit!*
reasonable [ˈriːznəbl] *hier: einleuchtend, plausibel*
get away [get əˈwei] *entkommen, -wischen*
at any rate [ˈeni reit] *auf jeden Fall, wenigstens*
mere [miə] *bloß*
most likely [məust ˈlaikli] *sehr wahrscheinlich*
decide *sich entschließen*
have a shot at s.th. [ʃɔt] *es mit et. versuchen*
recollect [rekəˈlekt] *sich erinnern (an)*
according to [əˈkɔːdiŋ] *zufolge, laut*
travel [ˈtrævl] *reisen*
notice [ˈnəutis] *bemerken, beobachten*
miss *übersehen*
enjoy doing s.th. [inˈdʒɔi] *daran Vergnügen finden, et. zu tun*
keep s.th. to o.s. [kiːp] *et. für sich behalten*
titbit of information [ˈtitbit, infəˈmeiʃən] *informatorischer Leckerbissen*
rang up [ræŋ] *von* ring up [riŋ] *anrufen*
colleague [ˈkɔliːg] *Kollege*
inspector [inˈspektə] *(Polizei)Inspektor, (-)Kommissar*
guffaw at s.o. [gʌˈfɔː] *j-n schallend auslachen*
by all means [miːnz] *hier: wenn Sie durchaus wollen*
be delighted *sich sehr freuen*
we are sick of F [sik] *hängt uns zum Hals heraus*
mad as a hatter [ˈhætə] *total verrückt*
complete [kəmˈpliːt] *vollständig, völlig*
print [print] *(ab)drucken*
have s.th. looked up [lukt] *et. nachschlagen lassen, hier: et. heraussuchen lassen*
right you are F *richtig!, jawohl!*

Wilson sent for his own °file of *The Times*, and looked up the letter of Mr. Acres-Noel. *The Times* had not thought it worth the honour of the middle page, but fortunately °had not degraded it into the °'Points' column.

'*Sir*,' it °ran,—

'*The °methods of the police in °dealing with the so-called Newton Mystery appear to show more than the usual °official °incompetence. As one of the passengers on the train on which Mr. Newton died, I have been °subjected to °considerable °annoyance—and I may add °compensated °in part by some °amusement—at the °fruitless and °irrelevant inquiries made by the police.*

'*It is °plain the police have no °notion of the °motives which °prompted the murder. Their inquiries show that. If they would °devote more attention to thinking what the motive was, and less to the °accumulation of useless information, the °apparent °complexity of the case would disappear. The truth is usually simple—too simple for idiots to see. Why was Newton murdered? Answer that, and it will appear plainly that only one person could have murdered him. Motive is °essentially °individual.*

'*I am, °yours, etc.*,

'*R. D. Acres-Noel.*'

°'Upon my word,' said Wilson to himself, 'that's a very °odd letter.'

He °read it several times over, staring at it as if the name of the murderer was written between the lines.

file [fail] *hier: abgelegte (Zeitungs)Nummern Pl*
had not degraded it into [di'greidid] *hier: hatte ihn nicht zum Erscheinen in ... erniedrigt*
points column [pɔints 'kɔləm] *Spalte mit kleinerem Schriftgrad, in der die Fortsetzungen der im vorderen Teil abgedruckten Artikel gebracht werden*
ran [ræn] *von* run [rʌn] *lauten, heißen*
method ['meθəd] *Methode*
deal with [di:l] *sich beschäftigen* od. *befassen mit*
official [ə'fiʃəl] *behördlich*
incompetence [in'kɔmpitəns] *Unfähigkeit*
subject to [səb'dʒekt] *aussetzen*
considerable [kən'sidərəbl] *erheblich, beträchtlich*
annoyance *Belästigung*
compensate ['kɔmpənseit] *entschädigen*
in part [pɑ:t] *teilweise*
amusement *Vergnügen*
fruitless ['fru:tlis] *fruchtlos*
irrelevant [i'relivənt] *irrelevant, nicht zur Sache gehörig*
plain [plein] *klar*
notion ['nəuʃən] *Vorstellung*
motive ['məutiv] *Motiv*
prompt [prɔmpt] *eingeben; hier: führen zu*
devote [di'vəut] *schenken*
accumulation [əkju:mju'leiʃən] *Anhäufung*
apparent [ə'pærənt] *scheinbar*
complexity [kəm'pleksiti] *Kompliziertheit, Schwierigkeit*
essentially [i'senʃəli] *in hohem Maße, ganz besonders*
individual [indi'vidjuəl] *persönlich(er Art)*
yours, etc. = Yours faithfully, Yours sincerely [jɔ:z, 'feiθfuli, sin'siəli] *Hochachtungsvoll*
upon my word [wə:d] *auf mein Wort!, hier: m-r Treu!, wahrhaftig!*
odd [ɔd] *merkwürdig, komisch*
read over [red] *von* read over [ri:d] *durchlesen*

Suddenly he leaped to his feet, and with an excitement he seldom showed, °dashed down °Whitehall to Inspector Blaikie's office. °Within ten minutes he was °making a proposition to that official which left him °starkly °incredulous.

'I know,' Wilson °persisted, °'it isn't a certainty, it's a thousand to one °chance. But it *is* a chance, and I want to try it. I'm not asking the °Department to °commit itself in any way, only to let me have °a couple of men °standing by. Don't you see, the whole °point about this °extraordinary letter is the way it °stresses the question of motive? And, more than that, it suggests that the writer knows what the motive was. Now, how could he do that unless—'

'But, if that's so, the man's mad!' Blaikie °protested. °'Whoever heard of anyone murdering a complete stranger just to *show* him?'

'Well, he certainly is mad, isn't he? You said so yourself, and his family's °notoriously crazy.'

°'He'll have to be °pretty well °off his rocker,' Blaikie °remarked, 'if he's to be kind enough to come and °shove his neck in a °noose for you.'

°'One can but try,' Wilson said. 'If you won't help me I'm going to try alone. I must have one shot at °getting to the bottom of it.' And °eventually Blaikie agreed.

The °upshot was that Wilson, °immediately after his °interview, °arranged

dash [dæʃ] *stürmen*
Whitehall [ˈwaitˈhɔːl] *Straße in London, Sitz der Ministerien*
within [wiˈðin] *innerhalb, binnen*
make a proposition [prɔpəˈziʃən] *e-e Behauptung aufstellen*
stark [stɑːk] *völlig*
incredulous [inˈkredjuləs] *ungläubig*
persist [pəˈsist] *beharren*
it isn't a certainty [ˈsəːtnti] *es ist nicht sicher*
chance *Wahrscheinlichkeit, Aussicht, Möglichkeit*
department [diˈpɑːtmənt] *hier: Polizeibehörde*
commit o.s. [kəˈmit] *sich binden* od. *festlegen*
a couple of F [ˈkʌpl] *ein paar*
stand by [stænd] *sich bereithalten*
point *springender Punkt*
extraordinary [iksˈtrɔːdnri] *ungewöhnlich, seltsam*
stress [stres] *betonen*
protest [prəˈtest] *protestieren*
whoever [hu(ː)ˈevə] *wer denn nur*
notorious [nəuˈtɔːriəs] *notorisch, wie jeder weiß*
he'll = he will
pretty well [ˈpriti] *ganz schön*
off one's rocker *sl.* [ˈrɔkə] *verrückt*
remark [riˈmɑːk] *bemerken*
shove [ʃʌv] *stecken*
noose [nuːs] *Schlinge*
one can but try [kæn, trai] *man kann es wenigstens versuchen*
get to the bottom of s.th. [ˈbɔtəm] *e-r Sache auf den Grund gehen*
eventually [iˈventʃuəli] *schließlich*
upshot [ˈʌpʃɔt] *Ergebnis, Ende*
immediately [iˈmiːdjətli] *unmittelbar, sofort*
interview [ˈintəvjuː] *Unterredung*
arrange [əˈreindʒ] *Vorkehrungen treffen, dafür sorgen (, daß)*

for the °posting of the following letter, °forged with °extreme care so as to °imitate the °handwriting of the °supposed °author. It was °dispatched from the °pillar-box nearest to Joseph Newton's Cornish cottage.

'*Dear Mr. Acres-Noel*,' it said,—

°'*Ever since our °chance meeting a few months ago, I have been thinking over the very interesting demonstration you were kind enough to give me °on that occasion. May I confess, however, that I am still not quite °satisfied; and I should be even more deeply °obliged if I could induce you to repeat it. °As it happens, I shall be returning to London this week-end, and °travelling down again to Cornwall on the Riviera express next Wednesday. If you too should °chance to be travelling that way, perhaps we may meet again.*

°'*Yours very truly,*

'*Joseph Newton.*'

Someone °remarkably °like the °late Joseph Newton settled himself comfortably in the corner of a first-class compartment in the Cornish Riviera express. He had the compartment to himself, and although the train had begun to °fill up, no other traveller had entered when the train °drew out of the station. Very °discreetly, passengers who came near it had been °warned away by the station officials.

The train had not yet °gathered its full speed when the °solitary traveller

posting ['pəustiŋ] *Absenden, Aufgeben*
forge [fɔːdʒ] *fälschen*
extreme care [iks'triːm kɛə] *größte Sorgfalt*
imitate ['imiteit] *nachahmen, -machen*
handwriting ['hændraitiŋ] *(Hand) Schrift*
supposed [sə'pəuzd] *vermeintlich, angeblich*
author ['ɔːθə] *Autor, Schriftsteller*
dispatch [dis'pætʃ] *abschicken*
pillar-box BE ['piləbɔks] *Briefkasten (in Säulenform)*
ever since ['evə sins] *seit(dem)*
chance meeting ['miːtiŋ] *zufälliges Zusammentreffen*
on that occasion [ə'keiʒən] *bei dieser Gelegenheit*
satisfied ['sætisfaid] *zufrieden*
be obliged [ə'blaidʒd] *zu Dank verpflichtet sein*
as it happens ['hæpənz] *wie es sich gerade trifft*
travel down to *(von London) abreisen* od. *abfahren nach*
chance to travel *zufällig reisen* od. *fahren*
Yours very truly ['truːli] *Hochachtungsvoll, Ihr sehr ergebener*
remarkable [ri'mɑːkəbl] *bemerkenswert, auffallend*
like [laik] *ähnlich (sehend)*
late [leit] *verstorben*
fill up [fil] *sich füllen*
drew out of [druː] *von* draw out of [drɔː] *hinausfahren aus, verlassen*
discreet [dis'kriːt] *diskret, unauffällig*
warn away = warn off [wɔːn] *fernhalten*
gather full speed ['gæðə] *Höchstgeschwindigkeit erreichen*
solitary ['sɔlitəri] *einsam*

°became conscious that someone was standing outside the compartment, and staring in at him. He raised his eyes from the magazine he was reading, and looked back. Slowly, the newcomer pushed back the °sliding door, entered the compartment, and sat down in the far corner.

He was a little old man, with a straggling beard, wearing very °shabby clothes. He flung down on the seat beside him a rug and a pillow °tied up in a strap. °Undoing his bundle, he settled himself with the pillow behind his head, the rug over his knees, and the strap on the seat beside him. Then he closed his eyes.

Wilson did and said nothing. It was °nervous work, waiting for his °cue. But by this time he knew he was right. °The millionth chance had °come off.

The train °flashed °at length—it seemed hours—through Maidenhead Station. Suddenly the old man spoke.

'Talking of murders,' he said, °'it is my turn to °apologize. I am afraid I °bungled it last time.'

°'Not at all,' said Wilson, hoping that his voice would not °give him away; 'but if you would °kindly just show me again how—'

°'With pleasure,' said the old man.

He moved °with alacrity to the corner opposite Wilson, took from his pocket a jewelled cigarette-case, and °proffered it. Wilson took a cigarette, and °did a second's rapid thinking before the match was °produced. A

became conscious [biˈkeim ˈkɔnʃəs] *von* become conscious [biˈkʌm] *gewahr werden, merken*

sliding door [ˈslaidiŋ dɔː] *Schiebetür*

shabby [ˈʃæbi] *schäbig, abgetragen*

tie up [tai] *zusammenbinden*

undo *öffnen, aufmachen*

nervous [ˈnəːvəs] *aufregend, beunruhigend*

cue [kjuː] *Stichwort*

the millionth chance [ˈmiljənθ] *die e-e Möglichkeit in e-r Million (von Möglichkeiten)*

come off [kʌm] *glücken, hier: eintreffen*

flash [flæʃ] *rasen*

at length [leŋθ] *endlich*

it is my turn [təːn] *es ist an mir*

apologize [əˈpɔlədʒaiz] *sich entschuldigen*

bungle [ˈbʌŋgl] *verpfuschen, -patzen*

not at all *durchaus nicht, keineswegs*

give away *verraten*

kindly [ˈkaindli] *freundlicherweise*

with pleasure [ˈpleʒə] *mit Vergnügen!*

with alacrity [əˈlækriti] *bereitwillig*

proffer [ˈprɔfə] *anbieten*

do a second's rapid thinking [ˈsekəndz, ˈθiŋkiŋ] *blitzschnell nachdenken*

produce [prəˈdjuːs] *hervor-, herausholen*

---

allow for *berücksichtigen*

turn out to be *sich herausstellen als*

no use [juːs] *zwecklos*

cigarette was something he had not °allowed for, and it might even °turn out to be poisoned. However, °no use to hesitate now. He °suffered Mr. Acres-Noel to light it, and the heavy °sweetish taste °confirmed his fears.

Fortunately, however, it was hardly °alight before the other rose and went to the window.

'You won't °mind my pulling down the blinds, will you?' he said; and Wilson °took advantage of his movement to °effect a °lightning exchange of the suspicious cigarette for one of his own. This was a relief, but clearly he must °show some signs of being affected by it. °Sleepiness seemed the °most likely °clue. He yawned.

'You °follow me so far, I °trust,' said the other.

'Perfectly,' said Wilson slowly. 'Please—°go—' Slowly his eyes closed, and his head began to °wag.

The old man seized the rug-strap.

'This is the next step,' he said, °attempting to °cast it over Wilson's head. But Wilson sprang to his feet, °warded off the strap, and °pressed a button beside him which had been °fixed °to communicate with the °adjoining compartment.

Almost as he °grappled with his now °frenzied °antagonist, two °stalwart policemen °in plain clothes °rushed in °to his aid. Mr. Acres-Noel, °alternately °protesting his innocence and °shrieking with wild laughter, was soon °safely secured. The train °slowed down and stopped at the °deserted

suffer ['sʌfə] *gestatten*
sweetish ['swi:tiʃ] *süßlich*
confirm [kən'fə:m] *bestätigen*
be alight [ə'lait] *brennen*
mind *et. haben gegen*
took advantage of s.th. [əd'vɑ:ntidʒ] *von* take advantage of s.th. *et. ausnutzen, sich et. zunutze machen*
effect [i'fekt] *vornehmen*
lightning ['laitniŋ] *blitzschnell*
show some signs of being affected by it [ʃəu, sainz, 'bi:iŋ, ə'fektid] *hier: irgendwie zeigen, daß sie wirkte*
sleepiness ['sli:pinis] *Schläfrigkeit*
most likely *wahrscheinlichst*
clue *Schlüssel (zum Erfolg)*
follow *folgen können, verstehen*
trust [trʌst] *hoffen*
go = go on [gəu] *fahren (Sie fort)!*
wag [wæg] *wackeln*
attempt [ə'tempt] *versuchen*
cast [kɑ:st] *werfen*
ward off [wɔ:d] *abwehren*
press a button [pres, 'bʌtn] *auf e-n Knopf drücken*
fix [fiks] *anbringen*
to communicate [kə'mju:nikeit] *hier: um e-e Verbindung herzustellen*
adjoining [ə'dʒɔiniŋ] *angrenzend, Nachbar…, Neben…*
grapple ['græpl] *ringen*
frenzied ['frenzid] *rasend, tobend*
antagonist [æn'tægənist] *Gegner, Widersacher*
stalwart ['stɔ:lwət] *kräftig*
in plain clothes [kləuðz] *in Zivil*
rush in [rʌʃ] *hereinstürzen*
(rushed) to his aid [rʌʃt, eid] … *und eilten ihm zu Hilfe*
alternately [ɔ:l'tə:nitli] *abwechselnd*
protest *beteuern*
shriek with laughter [ʃri:k, 'lɑ:ftə] *vor Lachen kreischen*
safely secured ['seifli si'kjuəd] *hier: in sicherem Gewahrsam*
slow down [sləu] *langsamer werden*
deserted [di'zə:tid] *verlassen*

station of Newbury °Racecourse, where °captors and °captive °descended almost °unnoticed. Then it sped upon its way.

Mr. Acres-Noel, °safe in °Broadmoor, has only one °complaint. The °authorities will not °supply him with Joseph Newton's new books. He wants to see whether that °popular °writer has °benefited by his lesson in practical °criminology.

racecourse [ˈreiskɔːs] *Rennbahn*
captors *Pl* [ˈkæptəz] *hier: die, die ihn gefangennahmen*
captive [ˈkæptiv] *hier: der Gefangene*
descend [diˈsend] *herabsteigen, hier: aussteigen*
unnoticed [ˈʌnˈnəutist] *unbemerkt, unbeobachtet*
safe [seif] *in sicherem Gewahrsam, sicher aufgehoben*
Broadmoor [ˈbrɔːdmuə] *Anstalt für kriminelle Geisteskranke in Berkshire, England* [ˈbɑːkʃiə]
complaint [kəmˈpleint] *Klage, Beschwerde*
authorities *Pl* [ɔːˈθɔritiz] *Behörde(n Pl)*
supply [səˈplai] *versorgen*
popular [ˈpɔpjulə] *beliebt*
writer [ˈraitə] *Schriftsteller, Autor*
benefit by [ˈbenifit] *Nutzen ziehen aus*
criminology [krimiˈnɔlədʒi] *Kriminologie, Wissenschaft vom Verbrechen*

The °Telltale Heart

By Edgar Allan Poe

°True!—°nervous—very, very °dreadfully nervous I had been and am; but why *will* you say that I am °mad? The °disease had °sharpened my senses—not °destroyed—not °dulled them. °Above all was the °sense of hearing °acute. I heard all things °in the heaven and in the earth. I heard many things in hell. How, then, am I mad? °Hearken! and °observe how °healthily—how calmly I can tell you the whole story.

It is impossible to say °how first the idea entered my brain; but once °conceived, it °haunted me day and night. °Object there was °none. °Passion there was none. I loved the old man. He had never °wronged me. He °had never given me insult. For his gold I had no desire. I think it was his eye! yes, it was this! One of his eyes °resembled that of a °vulture—a °pale blue eye, with a °film over it. Whenever it fell upon me, °my blood ran cold; and so °by degrees—very °gradually—I made up my mind to take the life of the old man, and °thus °rid myself of the eye for ever.

Now °this is the point. You °fancy me mad. °Madmen know nothing. But you should have seen *me*. You should have seen how °wisely I °proceeded—with what °caution—with what °fore-

telltale ['telteil] *verräterisch*
true [tru:] *zugegeben, freilich*
nervous ['nə:vəs] *nervös*
dreadful ['dredful] *furchtbar*
mad [mæd] *wahnsinnig, verrückt*
disease [di'zi:z] *Krankheit*
sharpen ['ʃɑ:pən] *schärfen*
destroy [dis'trɔi] *zerstören*
dull [dʌl] *abstumpfen*
above all [ə'bʌv ɔ:l] *vor allem*
sense of hearing ['hiəriŋ] *Gehör(sinn)*
acute [ə'kju:t] *hier: fein*
in (the) heaven and (in the) earth ['hevn, ə:θ] *im Himmel und auf Erden*
hearken! ['hɑ:kən] *(poetisch:) hör(en Sie) zu* od. *her!*
observe [əb'zə:v] *hier: sehen*
healthy ['helθi] *hier: geistig gesund, vernünftig*
how first the idea entered my brain [fə:st, ai'diə, 'entəd, brein] *wann und wie mir zuerst der Gedanke kam*
conceive [kən'si:v] *von* conceive an idea *auf e-n Gedanken kommen, hier: daraufkommen*
haunt [hɔ:nt] *verfolgen, quälen*
object ['ɔbdʒikt] *hier: Gegner*
none [nʌn] *kein(e)*
passion ['pæʃən] *Leidenschaft, heftige Gemütserregung*
wrong s.o. [rɔŋ] *j-n ungerecht behandeln, j-m Unrecht tun*
had given me insult ['givn, 'insʌlt] *von* give s.o. insult [giv] *j-n beleidigen*
resemble [ri'zembl] *gleichen*
vulture ['vʌltʃə] *Geier*
pale blue [peil blu:] *blaßblau*
film [film] *dünnes Häutchen, Film*
my blood ran cold [blʌd, ræn, kəuld] *das Blut erstarrte mir in den Adern*

sight—with what °dissimulation I went to work! I was never kinder to the old man than during the whole week before I killed him. And every night, about midnight, I turned the °latch of his door and opened it—oh, so gently! And then, when I had made an °opening °sufficient for my head, I put in a dark °lantern, all closed, closed, so that no light shone out, and then I °thrust in my head. Oh, you would have laughed to see how °cunningly I thrust it in! I moved it slowly—very, very slowly, so that I might not °disturb the old man's sleep. It °took me an hour to °place my whole head within the opening so far that I could see him as he lay upon his bed. Ha!—would a madman have been so wise as this? And then, when my head was well in the room, I °undid the lantern °cautiously—oh, so cautiously—cautiously (for the °hinges °creaked)—I undid it just so much that a °single thin °ray fell upon the vulture eye. And this I did for seven long nights—every night just at midnight—but I found the eye always closed; and so it was impossible to do the work; for it was not the old man who °vexed me, but his °Evil Eye. And every morning, when the day °broke, I went °boldly into the °chamber, and spoke °courageously to him, calling him by name in a hearty tone, and °inquiring how he had °passed the night. So you see he would have been a very °profound old man, indeed, to °suspect that every night, just at twelve, I looked in upon him while he slept.

by degrees [bai diˈgriːz] *nach u. nach*
gradual [ˈgrædʒuəl] *allmählich*
thus [ðʌs] *so*
rid o.s. of [rid] *sich befreien od. frei machen von*
this is the point [pɔint] *dies hier ist der springende Punkt*
fancy [ˈfænsi] *glauben*
madman [ˈmædmən] *Verrückte, Wahnsinnige*
wise [waiz] *klug*
proceed [prəˈsiːd] *vorgehen*
caution [ˈkɔːʃən] *Vorsicht*
foresight [ˈfɔːsait] *Vorsorge*

---

dissimulation [disimjuˈleiʃən] *Verstellung, Heuchelei*
latch [lætʃ] *hier: Türgriff*
opening [ˈəupniŋ] *Öffnung*
sufficient [səˈfiʃənt] *ausreichend, genügend*
lantern [ˈlæntən] *Laterne*
thrust [θrʌst] *stecken, schieben*
cunning [ˈkʌniŋ] *schlau, geschickt, listig*
disturb [disˈtəːb] *stören*
took me an hour [tuk, ˈauə] *von* take [teik] *dauern (Zeit), hier: ich brauchte e-e Stunde*
place [pleis] *hier: stecken*
undid [ˈʌnˈdid] *von* undo [ˈʌnˈduː] *aufmachen, öffnen*
cautious [ˈkɔːʃəs] *vorsichtig, behutsam*
hinge [hindʒ] *(Tür)Angel*
creak [kriːk] *quietschen*
single [ˈsiŋgl] *einzig*
ray [rei] *(Licht)Strahl*
vex [veks] *ärgern, irritieren*
evil eye [ˈiːvl ai] *böser Blick, hier: böses Auge*
broke [brəuk] *von* break [breik] *anbrechen*
bold [bəuld] *kühn, keck, dreist*
chamber [ˈtʃeimbə] *(veraltet:) Schlafzimmer*
courageous [kəˈreidʒəs] *beherzt, mutig*
inquire [inˈkwaiə] *sich erkundigen*
pass [pɑːs] *ver-, zubringen*
profound [prəˈfaund] *scharfsinnig*
suspect [səsˈpekt] *argwöhnen, den Verdacht haben*

Upon the eighth night I was more than usually cautious °in opening the door. A watch's minute hand moves more quickly than did mine. Never before that night had I *felt* the °extent of my own powers—of my °sagacity. I could scarcely °contain my feelings of triumph. To think that there I was, opening the door, °little by little, and he not even to dream of my °secret deeds or thoughts. I °fairly °chuckled at the idea; and perhaps he heard me; for he moved on the bed suddenly, as if °startled. Now you may think that I °drew back—but no. His room was °as black as pitch with the °thick darkness (for the °shutters were °close °fastened, °through fear of robbers), and so I knew that he could not see the opening of the door, and I °kept pushing it on °steadily, steadily.

I had my head in, and °was about to open the lantern, when my thumb °slipped upon the °tin °fastening, and the old man sprang up in the bed, crying out—"Who's there?"

I °kept quite still and said nothing. For a whole hour I did not move a muscle, and °in the meantime I did not hear him lie down. He was still sitting up in the bed listening;—just as I have done, night after night, °hearkening to the °death watches in the wall.

°Presently I heard a slight °groan, and I knew it was the groan of °mortal terror. It was not a groan of pain or of °grief—oh, no!—it was the °low °stifled °sound that °arises °from the

in opening *beim Öffnen*
extent [iksˈtent] *Ausmaß*
sagacity [səˈgæsiti] *Klugheit, Scharfsinn*
contain [kənˈtein] *zügeln*
little by little [ˈlitl] *(ganz) allmählich, nach u. nach*
secret [ˈsi:krit] *geheim*
fairly [ˈfɛəli] *geradezu, direkt*
chuckle [ˈtʃʌkl] *(stillvergnügt) in sich hineinlachen*
startled [ˈstɑ:tld] *aufgeschreckt*
drew back [dru: bæk] *von* draw back [drɔ:] *sich zurückziehen*
as black as pitch [pitʃ] *pechschwarz*
thick [θik] *hier: völlig*
shutter [ˈʃʌtə] *Fensterladen*
close [kləus] *fest, dicht*
fastened [ˈfɑ:snd] *ver-, geschlossen, verriegelt*
through fear of [θru: fiə] *aus Furcht vor*
kept pushing ... on [kept ˈpuʃiŋ] *von* keep pushing ... on [ki:p] *weiteraufdrükken*
steady [ˈstedi] *stetig, ständig; ruhig*
was about to [əˈbaut] *war im Begriff zu, wollte gerade*
slip [slip] *ausgleiten*
tin [tin] *Zinn..., Blech...*
fastening [ˈfɑ:sniŋ] *Verschluß*
kept still [stil] *von* keep still *sich ruhig verhalten*
in the meantime [ˈmi:ntaim] *hier: während der ganzen Zeit*
hearken to *horchen auf*
death watch [deθ] *Totenuhr (Klopfkäfer)*
presently [ˈprezntli] *bald darauf, dann*
groan [grəun] *Stöhnen*
mortal terror [ˈmɔ:tl ˈterə] *Todesangst*
grief [gri:f] *Kummer, Leid*
low [ləu] *leise*
stifled [ˈstaifld] *erstickt, unterdrückt*
sound [saund] *Ton, Laut*
arise [əˈraiz] *kommen*
from the bottom of the soul [ˈbɔtəm, səul] *aus tiefster Seele*

bottom of the soul when °overcharged with awe. I knew the sound well. °Many a night, just at midnight, when all the world slept, it has °welled up from my own °bosom, °deepening, with its dreadful °echo, the °terrors that °distracted me. I say I knew it well. I knew what the old man felt, and °pitied him, although I chuckled °at heart. I knew that he had been lying awake °ever since the first slight noise, when he had turned in the bed. His fears had been ever since °growing upon him. He had been trying to fancy them °causeless, but could not. He had been saying to himself—"It is °nothing but the wind in the °chimney—it is only a mouse crossing the floor," or "it is merely a °cricket which has made a single °chirp." Yes, he has been trying to °comfort himself with these °suppositions; but he had found all °in vain. *All in vain;* because Death, in approaching him, had °stalked with his black shadow before him, and °enveloped the °victim. And it was the °mournful °influence of the °unperceived shadow that caused him to feel —although he neither saw nor heard— to *feel* the presence of my head within the room.

When I had waited a long time, very patiently, without hearing him lie down, I °resolved to open a little—a very, very little °crevice in the lantern. So I opened it—you cannot °imagine how °stealthily, stealthily—until, °at length, a single °dim ray, like the °thread of the °spider, shot from out the crevice and full upon the vulture eye.

overcharged with awe ['əuvə'tʃɑ:dʒd, ɔ:] *hier: voller Furcht, furchtbeladen*
many a ... ['meni] *manch ...*
well up [wel] *aufsteigen*
bosom ['buzəm] *Busen, Brust, Herz*
deepen ['di:pən] *vertiefen, steigern*
echo ['ekəu] *Echo, Widerhall*
terror *(tödlicher) Schrecken, Entsetzen*
distract [dis'trækt] *quälen, peinigen*
I pitied him ['pitid] *er tat mir leid*
at heart [hɑ:t] *im Grunde (meines Herzens), im Innersten*
ever since ['evə sins] *seitdem*
grow upon [grəu] *Macht gewinnen über*
causeless ['kɔ:zlis] *grundlos, unbegründet*
nothing but ['nʌθiŋ] *nur*
chimney ['tʃimni] *Kamin, Schornstein*
cricket ['krikit] *Heimchen, Grille*
chirp [tʃə:p] *Gezirp*
comfort ['kʌmfət] *trösten, beruhigen*
supposition [sʌpə'ziʃən] *Vermutung*
in vain [vein] *vergebens, umsonst*
stalk [stɔ:k] *einherstolzieren*
envelop [in'veləp] *einhüllen, hier: (bereits) umklammern*
victim ['viktim] *Opfer*
mournful ['mɔ:nful] *düster*
influence ['influəns] *Einfluß, Macht*
unperceived ['ʌnpə'si:vd] *unbemerkt*

resolve [ri'zɔlv] *beschließen*
crevice ['krevis] *Spalt*
imagine [i'mædʒin] *sich vorstellen*
stealthy ['stelθi] *verstohlen*
at length [leŋθ] *endlich, schließlich*
dim [dim] *schwach, trüb*
thread [θred] *Faden*
spider ['spaidə] *Spinne*

It was open—wide, wide open—and I °grew °furious as I °gazed upon it. I saw it °with perfect distinctness—all a °dull blue, with a °hideous °veil over it that °chilled °the very marrow in my bones; but I could see nothing else of the old man's face or person: for I had °directed the ray as if °by instinct, °precisely upon the damned °spot.

And now have I not told you that what you mistake for madness is but °over-acuteness of the senses?—now, I say, there came to my ears a low, °dull, quick sound, such as a watch makes when enveloped in °cotton. I knew *that* sound well too. It was the °beating of the old man's heart. It °increased my °fury, as the beating of a °drum °stimulates the soldier into courage.

But even yet I °refrained and kept still. I scarcely breathed. I held the lantern °motionless. I tried how steadily I could °maintain the ray upon the eye. Meantime the °hellish °tattoo of the heart increased. It grew quicker and quicker, and louder and louder every °instant. The old man's terror *must* have been °extreme! It grew louder, I say, louder every moment!—do you °mark me well? I have told you that I am nervous: so I am. And now at the °dead hour of the night, °amid the dreadful silence of that old house, so strange a noise as this °excited me to °uncontrollable terror. Yet, for some minutes longer I refrained and stood still. But the beating grew louder, louder! I thought the heart

grew [gru:] *von* grow *werden*
furious ['fjuəriəs] *wütend, rasend*
gaze upon [geiz] *starren auf*
with perfect distinctness ['pə:fikt dis'tiŋktnis] *in aller Deutlichkeit, ganz klar*
dull [dʌl] *matt, trüb*
hideous ['hidiəs] *gräßlich, abscheulich*
veil [veil] *Schleier*
chill [tʃil] *frösteln* od. *erschauern lassen*
the very marrow in my bones ['mærəu, bəunz] *selbst das Mark in m-n Knochen, hier: mein Innerstes*
direct upon [di'rekt] *richten auf*
by instinct ['instiŋkt] *instinktiv*
precise [pri'sais] *genau*
spot [spɔt] *Stelle*
over-acuteness ['əuvərə'kju:tnis] *übergroße Schärfe*
dull *dumpf*
cotton ['kɔtn] *hier: Watte*
beating of the heart ['bi:tiŋ, hɑ:t] *Herzschlag*
increase [in'kri:s] *(sich) steigern* od. *vergrößern*
fury ['fjuəri] *Wut*
drum [drʌm] *Trommel*
stimulate s.o. into ['stimjuleit] *j-n anspornen zu*
refrain [ri'frein] *sich beherrschen* od. *zurückhalten*
motionless ['məuʃənlis] *unbeweglich, still*
maintain [mein'tein] *hier: richten*
hellish ['heliʃ] *höllisch, teuflisch*
tattoo [tə'tu:] *Klopfen, Trommeln*
instant ['instənt] *Augenblick*
extreme [iks'tri:m] *hier: ganz außergewöhnlich*
mark [mɑ:k] *sich merken, hier: zuhören*
dead [ded] *hier: ruhig*
amid [ə'mid] *(mitten) in*
excite to [ik'sait] *versetzen in*
uncontrollable [ʌnkən'trəuləbl] *unkontrollierbar, unbezähmbar*

must °burst. And now a new °anxiety °seized me—the sound would be heard by a neighbor! The old man's hour had come! With a loud °yell, I °threw open the lantern and leaped into the room. He °shrieked once—once only. °In an instant I °dragged him to the floor, and pulled the heavy bed over him. I then smiled gaily, to find the deed so far done. But, for many minutes, the heart beat on with a °muffled sound. This, however, did not vex me; it would not be heard through the wall. At length it °ceased. The old man was dead. I °removed the bed and °examined the °corpse. Yes, he was stone, °stone dead. I placed my hand upon the heart and held it there many minutes. There was no °pulsation. He was stone dead. His eye would °trouble me no more.

If still you think me mad, you will think so no longer when I °describe the wise °precautions I took for the °concealment of the °body. The night °waned, and I worked °hastily, but °in silence. First of all I °dismembered the corpse. I cut off the head and the arms and the legs.

I then took up three °planks from the °flooring of the chamber, and °deposited all between the °scantlings. I then °replaced the °boards so cleverly, so cunningly, that no human eye—not even his—could have °detected °any thing wrong. There was nothing to wash out—no °stain of any kind—no °blood-spot °whatever. I had been too °wary for that. A °tub had °caught all—ha! ha!

burst [bəːst] *zerspringen*
anxiety [æŋˈzaiəti] *Angst*
seize [siːz] *ergreifen, packen*
yell [jel] *(gellender) Schrei*
threw open [θruː] *von* throw open [θrəu] *aufreißen*
shriek [ʃriːk] *aufschreien*
in an instant *sofort, im Nu*
drag [dræg] *zerren*
muffled [ˈmʌfld] *gedämpft*
cease [siːs] *aufhören*
remove [riˈmuːv] *wegnehmen, entfernen*
examine [igˈzæmin] *untersuchen*
corpse [kɔːps] *Leiche*
stone dead [stəun] *mausetot*
pulsation [pʌlˈseiʃən] *Schlagen, Pochen*
trouble [ˈtrʌbl] *belästigen; quälen*
describe [disˈkraib] *beschreiben, schildern*
precautions I took [priˈkɔːʃənz] *von* take precautions *Vorsichtsmaßregeln* od. *Vorsorge treffen*
concealment [kənˈsiːlmənt] *Verbergen, Verstecken*
body [ˈbɔdi] *Leiche*
wane [wein] *zu Ende gehen*
hasty [ˈheisti] *hastig, schnell*
in silence [ˈsailəns] *schweigend*
dismember [disˈmembə] *zerstückeln*
plank [plæŋk] *Diele*
flooring [ˈflɔːriŋ] *Fußboden*
deposit [diˈpɔzit] *unterbringen*
scantling [ˈskæntliŋ] *Latte*
replace [riˈpleis] *wieder hinlegen* od. *einsetzen*
board [bɔːd] *Brett, Diele*
detect [diˈtekt] *entdecken, finden*
any thing = anything [ˈeniθiŋ]
stain [stein] *Fleck*
blood-spot *Blutfleck, -spritzer*
whatever [wɔtˈevə] *(nachgestellt u. mit vorausgehender Verneinung:) überhaupt kein, keinerlei*
wary [ˈwɛəri] *vor-, umsichtig*
tub [tʌb] *Zuber, Wanne*
caught [kɔːt] *von* catch [kætʃ] *auffangen*

When I °had made an end of these labors, it was four o'clock—still dark as midnight. As the bell °sounded the hour, there came a knocking at the street door. I went down to open it with a light heart,—for what had I *now* to fear? There entered three men, who introduced themselves, with perfect °suavity, as °officers of the police. A °shriek had been heard by a neighbor during the night; °suspicion of °foul play had been °aroused; °information had been lodged at the °police office, and they (the officers) had been °deputed to °search the °premises.

I smiled,—for *what* had I to fear? I °bade the gentlemen welcome. The shriek, I said, was my own in a dream. The old man, I °mentioned, was absent °in the country. I °took my visitors all over the house. I bade them search—search *well.* I led them, at length, to *his* chamber. I showed them his °treasures, °secure, °undisturbed. In the °enthusiasm of my °confidence, I brought chairs into the room, and °desired them *here* to rest from their °fatigues, while I myself, in the wild °audacity of my perfect triumph, °placed my own seat °upon the very spot beneath which °reposed the corpse of the victim.

The officers were °satisfied. My °*manner* had °convinced them. I was °singularly °at ease. They sat, and while I answered °cheerily, they °chatted °familiar things. But, °ere long, I felt myself °getting °pale and wished them gone. My head °ached, and I fancied a °ringing in my ears: but still

had made an end of s.th. *von* make an end of s.th. *mit et. Schluß machen, et. beenden*
sound the hour [saund] *die volle Stunde schlagen*
suavity [ˈswɑːviti] *Höflichkeit*
officer of the police [ˈɔfisə, pəˈliːs] *Polizeibeamte*
shriek [ʃriːk] *(gellender) Schrei*
suspicion [səsˈpiʃən] *Verdacht*
foul play [faul plei] *Verbrechen*
arouse [əˈrauz] *wecken, erregen*
information had been lodged [infəˈmeiʃən, lɔdʒd] *von* lodge information *Anzeige erstatten*
police office [ˈɔfis] = police station [ˈsteiʃən] *Polizeirevier*
depute [diˈpjuːt] *beauftragen*
search [səːtʃ] *durchsuchen*
premises *Pl* [ˈpremisiz] *hier: Haus, Räumlichkeiten Pl*
bade ... welcome [bæd ˈwelkəm] *von* bid s.o. welcome *j-n willkommen heißen*
mention [ˈmenʃən] *erwähnen*
in the country [ˈkʌntri] *auf dem Lande*
took *von* take *führen*
treasures *Pl* [ˈtreʒəz] *Reichtümer, Schätze*
secure [siˈkjuə] *sicher, in Sicherheit*
undisturbed [ˈʌndisˈtəːbd] *unangetastet, unberührt*
enthusiasm [inˈθjuːziæzəm] *hier: Überschwang*
confidence [ˈkɔnfidəns] *Selbstvertrauen; Dreistigkeit*
desire [diˈzaiə] *bitten, ersuchen*
fatigues *Pl* [fəˈtiːgz] *mühselige Arbeit, Strapaze*
audacity [ɔːˈdæsiti] *Kühnheit, Verwegenheit*
place *hier: stellen*
upon the very spot *auf eben jene Stelle*
repose [riˈpəuz] *ruhen*
satisfied [ˈsætisfaid] *zufrieden*
manner [ˈmænə] *Auftreten, Verhalten*
convince [kənˈvins] *überzeugen*
singularly [ˈsiŋgjuləli] *ungewöhnlich*
at ease [iːz] *entspannt, gelöst*

they sat and still chatted. The ringing °became more °distinct:—it °continued and became more distinct: I talked more °freely to °get rid of the feeling: but it continued and °gained °definitiveness—until, at length, I found that the noise was *not* within my ears.

No doubt I now grew *very* pale;—but I talked more °fluently, and with a °heightened voice. Yet the sound °increased—and what could I do? It was *a low, dull, quick sound—much such a sound as a watch makes when enveloped in cotton.* I °gasped for breath—and yet the officers heard it not. I talked more quickly—more °vehemently; but the noise steadily increased. I °arose and °argued about °trifles, °in a high key and with °violent °gesticulations, but the noise steadily increased. Why *would* they not be gone? I °paced the floor to and fro with heavy °strides, as if °excited to °fury by the °observation of the men—but the noise steadily increased. Oh God! what *could* I do? I °foamed—I °raved—I swore! I swung the chair upon which I had been sitting, and °grated it upon the boards, but the noise arose over all and °continually increased. It grew louder—louder—*louder!* And still the men chatted °pleasantly, and smiled. Was it possible they heard not? °Almighty God!—no, no! They heard!—they suspected!—they *knew!*—they were °making a mockery of my horror!—this I thought, and this I think. But any thing was better than this °agony! Any thing was more °tolerable than this °derision! I could °bear those

cheery [ˈtʃiəri] *vergnügt, munter*
chat [tʃæt] *(veraltet:)* = chatter [ˈtʃætə] *plaudern (über)*
familiar [fəˈmiljə] *bekannt, vertraut*
ere long [ɛə lɔŋ] *(poetisch:) bald*
get [get] *werden*
pale [peil] *blaß, bleich*
ache [eik] *weh tun, schmerzen*
ringing [ˈriŋiŋ] *Klingen*

---

became [biˈkeim] *von* become [biˈkʌm] *werden*
distinct [disˈtiŋkt] *deutlich, klar*
continue [kənˈtinju:] *andauern, anhalten*
freely [ˈfri:li] *ungehemmt, hier: viel*
get rid of *loswerden*
gain [gein] *gewinnen, erlangen*
definitiveness [diˈfinitivnis] *Endgültigkeit, Wirklichkeit*
fluent [ˈflu:ənt] *fließend*
heightened [ˈhaitnd] *hier: erhoben*
increase *zunehmen*
gasp for breath [gɑ:sp, breθ] *nach Luft ringen*
vehement [ˈvi:imənt] *heftig*
arose [əˈrəuz] *von* arise [əˈraiz] *aufstehen, sich erheben*
argue [ˈɑ:gju:] *debattieren, streiten*
trifle [ˈtraifl] *Kleinigkeit*
in a high key [hai ki:] *in hohem Ton(fall), hier: schrill*
violent [ˈvaiələnt] *heftig*
gesticulation [dʒestikjuˈleiʃən] *Gesten Pl*
pace the floor to and fro [peis, flɔ:, frəu] *im Zimmer auf u. ab gehen*
stride [straid] *(großer) Schritt*
excite *reizen, hier: bringen*
fury *Raserei*
observation [ɔbzə(:)ˈveiʃən] *Bemerkung*
foam [fəum] *schäumen (vor Wut)*
rave [reiv] *rasen, toben*
grate it upon [greit] *hier: damit knirschend fahren über*
continual [kənˈtinjuəl] *fortwährend*

°hypocritical smiles no longer! I felt that I must °scream or die!—and now—again!—hark! louder! louder! louder! *louder!*—

°"Villains!" I shrieked, °"dissemble no more! I °admit the deed!—°tear up the planks!—here, here!—it is the beating of his hideous heart!"

pleasant ['pleznt] *freundlich, nett*
Almighty God! [ɔːl'maiti gɔd] *Allmächtiger Gott!*
make a mockery of ['mɔkəri] *Spott treiben mit*
agony ['ægəni] *(Höllen)Qual*
tolerable ['tɔlərəbl] *erträglich*
derision [di'riʒən] *Hohn, Spott*
bear [bɛə] *ertragen*

---

hypocritical [hipəu'kritikəl] *heuchlerisch, scheinheilig*
scream [skriːm] *schreien, kreischen*
villain ['vilən] *Schurke*
dissemble [di'sembl] *sich verstellen*
admit [əd'mit] *zugeben, gestehen*
tear up [tɛə] *herausreißen*

The °Cask of °Amontillado

By Edgar Allan Poe

The thousand °injuries of Fortunato I had °borne as I best could, but when he °ventured upon °insult, I vowed °revenge. You, who so well know the nature of my soul, will not suppose, however, that I °gave utterance to a threat. °*At length* I would be °avenged; this was a point °definitely °settled—but °the very °definitiveness with which it was °resolved, °precluded the idea of risk. I must not only punish, but punish °with impunity. A °wrong is °unredressed when °retribution overtakes its °redresser. It is equally unredressed when the °avenger °fails to °make himself felt as such to him who has done the wrong.

It must be understood that neither by word nor deed had I given Fortunato cause to doubt my °good will. I continued as was my °wont, to smile in his face, and he did not °perceive that my smile *now* was at the thought of his °immolation.

He had a °weak point—this Fortunato—although in other °regards he was a man to be respected and even feared. He °prided himself on his °connoisseurship in wine. Few Italians have the true °virtuoso °spirit. For the most part their enthusiasm is °adapted to °suit the time and opportunity—to °practise imposture upon the British and Austrian millionaires. In paint-

cask [kɑːsk] *Faß*
amontillado [əmɔntiˈlɑːdəu] *Amontillado (heller, herber Sherry)*
injury [ˈindʒəri] *Kränkung*
borne [bɔːn] *von* bear [bɛə] *ertragen, erdulden*
venture [ˈventʃə] *(es) wagen*
insult [ˈinsʌlt] *persönliche Beleidigung*
revenge [riˈvendʒ] *Rache*
gave utterance to [geiv ˈʌtərəns] *von* give utterance to [giv] *aussprechen, äußern*
at length [leŋθ] *schließlich*
avenge [əˈvendʒ] *rächen*
definitely [ˈdefinitli] *endgültig*
settled [ˈsetld] *beschlossen*
the very ... *gerade die ...*
definitiveness [diˈfinitivnis] *Entschiedenheit*
resolve [riˈzɔlv] *beschließen*
preclude [priˈkluːd] *ausschließen*
with impunity [imˈpjuːniti] *(hier: selbst) ungestraft*
wrong [rɔŋ] *Unrecht*
unredressed [ˈʌnriˈdrest] *nicht vergolten, ungesühnt*
retribution [retriˈbjuːʃən] *Vergeltung, Bestrafung*
redresser [riˈdresə] *der das Unrecht Wiedergutmachende*
avenger [əˈvendʒə] *Rächer*
fail to do s.th. [feil] *etwas nicht fertigbringen*
make o.s. felt as ... *es j-n fühlen lassen, daß man ... ist*
good will [gud wil] *Wohlwollen*
wont [wəunt] *Gewohnheit, Art*
perceive [pəˈsiːv] *(be)merken*
immolation [iməuˈleiʃən] *Opferung*
weak point [wiːk pɔint] *schwache Stelle, Schwäche*
regard [riˈgɑːd] *Hinsicht*
pride o.s. on s.th. [praid] *stolz sein auf etwas*

ing and °gemmary Fortunato, like his countrymen, was a °quack—but in the matter of old wines he was °sincere. °In this respect I did not °differ from him °materially: I was °skilful in the Italian °vintages myself, and bought largely whenever I could.

It was about °dusk, one evening during the °supreme madness of the °carnival season, that I °encountered my friend. He °accosted me with °excessive °warmth, for he had been drinking much. The man wore °motley. He had on a °tight-fitting °parti-striped dress, and his head was °surmounted by the °conical cap and bells. I was so pleased to see him, that I thought I should never °have done °wringing his hand.

I said to him: "My dear Fortunato, °you are luckily met. How remarkably well you are looking today! But I have received a °pipe of what °passes for Amontillado, and I have my doubts."

"How?" said he. "Amontillado? A pipe? Impossible! And in the middle of the carnival!"

"I have my doubts," I replied; "and I was silly enough to pay the full Amontillado price without °consulting you in the matter. You were °not to be found, and I was °fearful of °losing a °bargain."

"Amontillado!"

"I have my doubts."

"Amontillado!"

"And I must satisfy them."

"Amontillado!"

connoisseurship [kɔnəˈsəːʃip] *Kennerschaft*
virtuoso [vəːtjuˈəuzəu] *Kunstliebhaber*
spirit [ˈspirit] *Einstellung*
be adapted [əˈdæptid] *angewendet werden*
suit [sjuːt] *sich anpassen*
practise imposture upon s.o. [ˈpræktis imˈpɔstʃə] *j-n betrügen* od. *hereinlegen*

---

gemmary [ˈdʒeməri] *(Gebiet der) Edelsteine*
quack [kwæk] *prahlerischer Dilettant, Scharlatan*
sincere [sinˈsiə] *aufrichtig, hier: ernst zu nehmen*
in this respect *in dieser Hinsicht*
differ from [ˈdifə] *sich unterscheiden von*
materially [məˈtiəriəli] *wesentlich*
be skilful in [ˈskilful] *sich verstehen auf*
vintage [ˈvintidʒ] *guter Wein*
dusk [dʌsk] *Abenddämmerung*
supreme [sjuːˈpriːm] *größt*
carnival season [ˈkɑːnivəl ˈsiːzn] *Karnevalszeit*
encounter s.o. [inˈkauntə] *j-n treffen, j-m begegnen*
accost s.o. [əˈkɔst] *j-n ansprechen* od. *begrüßen*
excessive [ikˈsesiv] *übertrieben*
warmth [wɔːmθ] *Herzlichkeit*
motley [ˈmɔtli] *Narrenkostüm*
tight-fitting [ˈtaitfitiŋ] *enganliegend*
parti-striped [ˈpɑːtistraipt] *buntgestreift*
surmounted [səːˈmauntid] *bedeckt*
conical [ˈkɔnikəl] *spitz*
have done doing s.th. *mit etwas aufhören*
wring s.o.'s hand [riŋ] *j-m die Hand drücken*
you are luckily met *welch ein Glück, Sie zu treffen*
pipe [paip] *großes Weinfaß*
pass for s.th. [pɑːs] *angeblich etwas sein, etwas sein sollen*
consult [kənˈsʌlt] *zu Rate ziehen, um Rat fragen*

"As you are °engaged, I am on my way to Luchesi. If anyone has a °critical turn, it is he. He will tell me—"

"Luchesi cannot °tell Amontillado from Sherry."

"And yet some fools °will have it that his °taste is a °match for your own."

"Come, let us go."

°"Whither?"

"To your °vaults."

"My friend, no; I will not °impose upon your good nature. I perceive you have an °engagement. Luchesi—"

"I have no engagement; come."

"My friend, no. It is not the engagement, but the °severe cold with which I perceive you are °afflicted. The vaults are °insufferably damp. They are °encrusted with °nitre."

"Let us go, nevertheless. The cold is merely nothing. Amontillado! You have been imposed upon. And °as for Luchesi, he cannot °distinguish Sherry from Amontillado."

°Thus speaking, Fortunato °possessed himself of my arm. Putting on a mask of black silk, and °drawing a °*roquelaire* closely about my person, I °suffered him to °hurry me to my palazzo.

There were no °attendants at home; they had °absconded to °make merry °in honour of the time. I had told them that I should not return until the morning, and had given them °explicit °orders not to °stir from the house. These orders were °sufficient, I well

not to be found [faund] *nicht zu finden*
be fearful [ˈfiəful] *Angst haben, fürchten*
lose [lu:z] *kommen um*
bargain [ˈbɑ:gin] *gutes Geschäft, Gelegenheitskauf*

---

be engaged [inˈgeidʒd] *etwas vorhaben, keine Zeit haben*
have a critical turn [ˈkritikəl tə:n] *hier: sich auskennen*
tell s.th. from s.th. *etwas von etwas unterscheiden können*
s.o. will have it that *j-d behauptet, daß*
taste [teist] *Geschmackssinn*
be a match for s.o. [mætʃ] *es mit j-m aufnehmen können*
whither [ˈwiðə] *wohin*
vault [vɔ:lt] *Weinkeller, Kellergewölbe*
impose upon s.o.'s good nature [imˈpəuz, ˈneitʃə] *j-s Gutmütigkeit ausnützen*
engagement [inˈgeidʒmənt] *Verabredung*
severe cold [siˈviə kəuld] *starke Erkältung*
be afflicted with [əˈfliktid] *leiden an*
insufferable [inˈsʌfərəbl] *unerträglich*
be encrusted [inˈkrʌstid] *bedeckt sein*
nitre [ˈnaitə] *Salpeter*
as for ... *was ... anbetrifft*
distinguish [disˈtiŋgwiʃ] *unterscheiden*
thus [ðʌs] *so, auf diese Art*
possess o.s. of s.th. [pəˈzes] *hier: etwas ergreifen*
draw s.th. about one [drɔ:] *etwas um sich hüllen*
roquelaire [rɔkəˈlɛə] *weiter Mantel*
suffer s.o. to do s.th. [ˈsʌfə] *j-n etwas tun lassen*
hurry [ˈhʌri] *drängen*
attendant [əˈtendənt] *Diener; Pl Dienerschaft*
abscond [əbˈskɔnd] *sich heimlich davonmachen*
make merry [ˈmeri] *lustig sein, sich amüsieren*
in honour of the time [ˈɔnə] *hier: wie es sich zu dieser Zeit gehört*

knew, to °insure their °immediate °disappearance, °one and all, as soon as my back was turned.

I took from their °sconces two °flambeaux, and giving one to Fortunato, °bowed him through several °suites of rooms to the °archway that led into the vaults. I °passed down a long and °winding staircase, °requesting him to be °cautious as he followed. We came at length to the °foot of the descent, and stood together on the damp ground of the °catacombs of the Montresors.

The °gait of my friend was °unsteady, and the bells upon his cap °jingled as he °strode.

"The pipe?" said he.

"It is °further on," said I; "but °observe the white °webwork which °gleams from these °cavern walls."

He °turned towards me, and looked into my eyes with two °filmy °orbs that °distilled the °rheum of °intoxication.

"Nitre?" he asked, at length.

"Nitre!" I replied. "How long have you had that °cough?"

"Ugh! ugh! ugh!—ugh! ugh! ugh!—ugh! ugh! ugh!—ugh! ugh! ugh!—ugh! ugh! ugh!"

My poor friend found it impossible to reply for many minutes.

"It is nothing," he said, °at last.

"Come," I said, with °decision, "we will go back; your health is °precious. You are rich, respected, °admired, °beloved; you are happy, as once I was.

explicit [iksˈplisit] *ausdrücklich*
order [ˈɔːdə] *Befehl*
stir [stəː] *sich rühren*
be sufficient [səˈfiʃənt] *genügen*

---

insure [inˈʃuə] *garantieren*
immediate [iˈmiːdjət] *sofortig*
disappearance [disəˈpiərəns] *Verschwinden*
one and all *ohne Ausnahme*
sconce [skɔns] *Halter*
flambeau [ˈflæmbəu] *Fackel*
bow s.o. through s.th. [bau] *j-n unter Verbeugungen durch etwas geleiten*
suite of rooms [swiːt] *Zimmerflucht*
archway [ˈɑːtʃwei] *Bogengang*
pass down [pɑːs] *hinuntergehen*
winding staircase [ˈwaindiŋ ˈstɛəkeis] *Wendeltreppe*
request [riˈkwest] *bitten*
cautious [ˈkɔːʃəs] *vorsichtig*
foot of the descent [diˈsent] *unteres Ende der Treppe*
catacomb [ˈkætəkuːm] *Katakombe*
gait [geit] *Gang*
unsteady [ˈʌnˈstedi] *unsicher, schwankend, wackelig*
jingle [ˈdʒiŋgl] *klingeln*
strode [strəud] *von* stride [straid] *steif gehen, stelzen*
further on [ˈfəːðə] *weiter vorn*
observe [əbˈzəːv] *ansehen*
webwork [ˈwebwəːk] *Flor, pelzartige Oberfläche*
gleam [gliːm] *schimmern*
cavern [ˈkævən] *Höhle*
turn towards s.o. [təːn təˈwɔːdz] *sich zu j-m umdrehen*
filmy [ˈfilmi] *verschleiert, trübe*
orb [ɔːb] *(poetisch:) Auge*
distill [disˈtil] *herauströpfeln lassen*
rheum [ruːm] *Tränen, Wasser*
intoxication [intɔksiˈkeiʃən] *Trunkenheit*
cough [kɔf] *Husten*

at last [lɑːst] *schließlich, endlich*
decision [diˈsiʒən] *Entschiedenheit*
precious [ˈpreʃəs] *kostbar*
admired [ədˈmaiəd] *bewundert*
beloved [biˈlʌvd] *geliebt*

You are a man to be °missed. °For me it is no matter. We will go back; you will be ill, and I cannot be °responsible. °Besides, there is Luchesi—"

"Enough," he said; "the cough is a mere nothing; it will not kill me. I shall not °die of a cough."

"True—true," I replied; "and, °indeed, I had no °intention of °alarming you unnecessarily—but you should use all °proper °precautions. A °draught of this °Medoc will °defend us from the damps."

Here I °knocked off the °neck of a bottle which I drew from a long row of its °fellows that lay upon the °mould.

"Drink," I said, °presenting him the wine.

He raised it to his lips with a °leer. He °paused and nodded to me °familiarly, while his bells jingled.

"I drink," he said, "to the °buried that °repose around us."

"And I to your long life."

He again took my arm, and we °proceeded.

"These vaults," he said, "are °extensive."

"The Montresors," I replied, "were a °great and numerous family."

"I forget your °arms."

"A °huge °human foot °d'or, in a °field °azure; the foot °crushes a °serpent °rampant whose °fangs are °imbedded in the °heel."

"And the °motto?"

°"*Nemo me impune lacessit.*"

"Good!" he said.

miss [mis] *vermissen*
for me it is no matter *mir macht es nichts aus*
responsible [ris'pɔnsəbl] *verantwortlich*
besides [bi'saidz] *außerdem*

die of [dai] *sterben an*
indeed [in'di:d] *bestimmt*
intention [in'tenʃən] *Absicht*
alarm [ə'lɑ:m] *beunruhigen*
proper ['prɔpə] *geeignet*
precaution [pri'kɔ:ʃən] *Vorsichtsmaßnahme*
draught [drɑ:ft] *Schluck*
Medoc ['medɔk] *Medoc (französische Weinsorte)*
defend s.o. from [di'fend] *j-n schützen vor*
knock off [nɔk] *abschlagen*
neck of a bottle *Flaschenhals*
fellows *Pl* ['feləuz] *hier: gleichartige Flaschen, Flaschen derselben Sorte*
mould [məuld] *Sims*
present s.o. s.th. [pri'zent] *j-m etwas reichen*
leer [liə] *gieriger Blick*
pause [pɔ:z] *innehalten*
familiar [fə'miljə] *vertraulich*
the buried ['berid] *die Begrabenen*
repose [ri'pəuz] *ruhen, begraben sein*
proceed [prə'si:d] *weitergehen*
extensive [iks'tensiv] *ausgedehnt, groß*
great [greit] *bedeutend*
arms *Pl* [ɑ:mz] *Wappen*
huge [hju:dʒ] *sehr groß, riesig*
human ['hju:mən] *menschlich*
d'or [dɔ:] *(französisch:) golden*
field [fi:ld] *Feld, Grundfläche*
azure ['æʒə] *azurblau, azurn*
crush [krʌʃ] *zertreten*
serpent ['sə:pənt] *Schlange*
rampant ['ræmpənt] *aufgerichtet*
fang [fæŋ] *Giftzahn*
be imbedded in [im'bedid] *vergraben sein in*
heel [hi:l] *Ferse*
motto ['mɔtəu] *Motto, Sinnspruch*
Nemo me impune lacessit! *Niemand fordert mich ungestraft heraus!*

The wine °sparkled in his eyes and the bells jingled. My own °fancy °grew warm with the Medoc. We °passed through walls of °piled °bones, with casks and °puncheons °intermingling, into the °inmost °recesses of the catacombs. I paused again, and this time I °made bold to °seize Fortunato by an arm above the elbow.

"The nitre," I said; "see, it °increases. It hangs like moss upon the vaults. We are below the river's bed. The drops of °moisture °trickle among the bones. Come, we will go back °ere it is too late. Your cough—"

"It is nothing," he said; "let us go on. But first, another draught of the Medoc."

I °broke and reached him a °flagon of De Grave. He °emptied it °at a breath. His eyes °flashed with a °fierce °light. He laughed and threw the bottle °upward with a °gesticulation I did not understand.

I looked at him °in surprise. He °repeated the °movement—a °grotesque one.

"You do not °comprehend?" he said.

"Not I," I replied.

"Then you are not of the °brotherhood."

"How?"

"You are not of the °masons."

"Yes, yes," I said; "yes, yes."

"You? Impossible! A mason?"

"A mason," I replied.

"A °sign," he said.

"It is this," I answered, °producing a °trowel from beneath the °folds of my *roquelaire*.

sparkle ['spɑ:kl] *funkeln*
fancy ['fænsi] *Phantasie*
grew warm [gru:] *von* grow warm [grəu] *angestachelt werden*
pass through [pɑ:s θru:] *hier: vorbeigehen an*
piled [paild] *aufgestapelt*
bone [bəun] *Knochen; Pl Gebeine*
puncheon ['pʌntʃən] *großes Weinfaß*
intermingling [intə(:)'miŋgliŋ] *dazwischen verteilt*
inmost ['inməust] *tiefst, innerst*
recess [ri'ses] *Winkel; Tiefe*
make bold [bəuld] *es wagen*
seize [si:z] *ergreifen, fassen*
increase [in'kri:s] *zunehmen*
moisture ['mɔistʃə] *Feuchtigkeit*
trickle ['trikl] *sickern*
ere [εə] *(poetisch:) ehe, bevor*

broke [brəuk] *von* break [breik] *hier: anbrechen*
flagon ['flægən] *bauchige Flasche*
empty ['empti] *leeren*
at a breath [breθ] *auf e-n Zug*
flash [flæʃ] *blitzen*
fierce [fiəs] *wild, leidenschaftlich*
light [lait] *hier: Feuer*
upward ['ʌpwəd] *hoch*
gesticulation [dʒestikju'leiʃən] *Gebärde, lebhafte Geste*
in surprise [sə'praiz] *überrascht, verwundert*
repeat [ri'pi:t] *wiederholen*
movement ['mu:vmənt] *Bewegung*
grotesque [grəu'tesk] *grotesk, seltsam*
comprehend [kɔmpri'hend] *verstehen*
brotherhood ['brʌðəhud] *Bruderschaft*
mason ['meisn] *Freimaurer; Maurer*
sign [sain] *Zeichen, Erkennungs-, Geheimzeichen*
produce [prə'dju:s] *hervorholen, herausziehen*
trowel ['trauəl] *Maurerkelle*
fold [fəuld] *Falte*

"You °jest," he exclaimed, °recoiling a few °paces. "But let us proceed to the Amontillado."

°"Be it so," I said, °replacing the °tool beneath the cloak, and again offering him my arm. He leaned upon it heavily. We continued our route °in search of the Amontillado. We passed through a °range of low °arches, °descended, °passed on, and descending again, °arrived at a deep °crypt, in which the °foulness of the air caused our flambeaux °rather to glow than °flame.

At the °most remote end of the crypt there °appeared another °less spacious. Its walls had been °lined with °human remains, °piled to the vault °overhead, °in the fashion of the great catacombs of Paris. Three sides of this °interior crypt were °still °ornamented in this manner. From the fourth the bones had been thrown down, and lay °promiscuously upon the earth, forming at one point a °mound °of some size. Within the wall thus °exposed by the °displacing of the bones, we perceived a °still interior recess, in °depth °about four feet, in °width three, in height six or seven. It seemed to have been °constructed for no special °use within itself, but formed °merely the °interval between two of the °colossal °supports of the roof of the catacombs, and was °backed by one of their °circumscribing walls of °solid °granite.

It was °in vain that Fortunato, °uplifting his °dull °torch, °endeavoured to °pry into the depth of the

jest [dʒest] *spotten*
recoil [ri'kɔil] *zurückweichen*
pace [peis] *Schritt*
be it so *gut, einverstanden*
replace [ri'pleis] *(wieder) zurückstecken*
tool [tu:l] *Werkzeug*
in search of [sə:tʃ] *auf der Suche nach*
range [reindʒ] *Reihe*
arch [ɑ:tʃ] *(Gewölbe) Bogen*
descend [di'send] *hinuntergehen, tiefer steigen*
pass on *weitergehen*
arrive at [ə'raiv] *gelangen zu*
crypt [kript] *Gruft*
foulness of the air ['faulnis, εə] *schlechte, sauerstoffarme Luft*
rather ['rɑ:ðə] *eher*
flame [fleim] *lodern, flammen*
most remote [məust ri'məut] *entferntest, entlegenst, äußerst*
appear [ə'piə] *sichtbar werden*
less spacious ['speiʃəs] *weniger groß, kleiner*
line [lain] *einfassen*
human remains *Pl* [ri'meinz] *menschliche Überreste*
pile [pail] *aufschichten*
overhead ['əuvə'hed] *oben*
in the fashion of ['fæʃən] *im Stil von, (ähnlich) wie*
interior [in'tiəriə] *inner*
still [stil] *noch*
ornamented ['ɔ:nəmentid] *verziert, geschmückt*
promiscuously [prə'miskjuəsli] *kunterbunt durcheinander*
mound [maund] *Haufen, Berg*
of some size [saiz] *von beträchtlicher Größe, ziemlich groß*
expose [iks'pəuz] *freilegen*
displace [dis'pleis] *verlagern*
still interior *noch verborgener gelegen*
depth [depθ] *Tiefe*
about [ə'baut] *etwa, ungefähr*
width [widθ] *Breite*
construct [kən'strʌkt] *bauen*
use within itself [ju:s] *Selbstzweck*
merely ['miəli] *nur, lediglich*
interval ['intəvəl] *Zwischenraum*
colossal [kə'lɔsl] *riesig*
support [sə'pɔ:t] *Stützpfeiler*

recess. Its °termination the feeble light did not °enable us to see.

"Proceed," I said; "herein is the Amontillado. As for Luchesi—"

"He is an °ignoramus," interrupted my friend, as he stepped unsteadily forward, while I °followed °immediately at his heels. °In an instant he had °reached the °extremity of the °niche, and finding his °progress °arrested by the rock, stood °stupidly °bewildered. °A moment more and I had °fettered him to the granite. In its surface were two iron °staples, °distant from each other about two feet, °horizontally. From one of these °depended a short °chain, from the other a °padlock. Throwing the °links about his °waist, it was but the work of a few seconds to °secure it. He was too much °astounded to °resist. °Withdrawing the key I stepped back from the recess.

°"Pass your hand," I said, "over the wall; you °cannot help feeling the nitre. Indeed it is *very* damp. °Once more let me °*implore* you to return. No? Then I must °positively leave you. But I must first °render you all the little attentions in my power."

"The Amontillado!" °ejaculated my friend, °not yet °recovered from his °astonishment.

"True," I replied; "the Amontillado."

As I said these words I °busied myself among the °pile of bones of which I have before spoken. Throwing them °aside, I soon °uncovered a °quantity of °building stones and °mortar. With these °materials and °with the aid of my trowel, I began

back [bæk] *den Hintergrund bilden*
circumscribing [ˈsəːkəmskraibiŋ] *außen herumführend*
solid [ˈsɔlid] *massiv*
granite [ˈgrænit] *Granit*
in vain [vein] *vergeblich*
uplift [ʌpˈlift] *hochhalten*
dull [dʌl] *schwach, trübe*
torch [tɔːtʃ] *Fackel*
endeavour [inˈdevə] *versuchen*
pry into [prai] *zu erforschen suchen*

---

termination [təːmiˈneiʃən] *(äußerstes) Ende*
enable s.o. [iˈneibl] *es j-m möglich machen*
ignoramus [ignəˈreiməs] *Ignorant*
follow s.o. at his heels [ˈfɔləu] *j-m auf den Fersen folgen*
immediately [iˈmiːdjətli] *sofort*
in an instant [ˈinstənt] *im Nu*
reach *erreichen, gelangen zu*
extremity [iksˈtremiti] *äußerstes Ende*
niche [nitʃ] *Nische*
progress [ˈprəugres] *Weitergehen, Weitervordringen*
arrest [əˈrest] *aufhalten*
stupid [ˈstjuːpid] *einfältig*
bewildered [biˈwildəd] *verwirrt*
a moment more and ... [ˈməumənt] *im nächsten Moment ...*
fetter [ˈfetə] *fesseln*
staple [ˈsteipl] *Krampe*
distant [ˈdistənt] *entfernt*
horizontal [hɔriˈzɔntl] *horizontal, waagerecht*
depend [diˈpend] *herabhängen*
chain [tʃein] *Kette*
padlock [ˈpædlɔk] *Vorhängeschloß*
links *Pl* [liŋks] *Fessel*
waist [weist] *Taille*
secure [siˈkjuə] *hier: schließen*
astounded [əsˈtaundid] *verblüfft*
resist [riˈzist] *Widerstand leisten*
withdraw [wiðˈdrɔː] *herausziehen*
pass one's hand over *mit der Hand fahren über*

°vigorously to °wall up the entrance of the niche.

I had scarcely laid the first °tier of the °masonry when I discovered that the intoxication of Fortunato had °in a great measure °worn off. The earliest °indication I had of this was a °low °moaning cry from the depth of the recess. It was *not* the cry of a drunken man. There was then a long and °obstinate silence. I laid the second tier, and the third, and the fourth; and then I heard the °furious °vibrations of the chain. The noise °lasted for several minutes, during which, that I might °hearken to it with the more °satisfaction, I °ceased my labours and sat down upon the bones. When at last the °clanking °subsided, I °resumed the trowel, and finished without °interruption the fifth, the sixth, and the seventh tier. The wall was now °nearly °upon a level with my breast. I again paused, and holding the flambeaux over the mason-work, threw a few feeble °rays upon the figure within.

A °succession of loud and °shrill °screams, °bursting suddenly from the throat of the °chained form, seemed to °thrust me °violently back. For a °brief moment I °hesitated—I °trembled. °Unsheathing my °rapier, I began to °grope with it about the recess; but the thought of an °instant °reassured me. I placed my hand upon the solid °fabric of the catacombs, and felt satisfied. I °reapproached the wall. I replied to the °yells of him who °clamoured. I °re-echoed—I °aided—I °surpassed them

s.o. cannot help doing s.th. *j-d muß etwas tun*
once more *noch einmal*
implore [im'plɔ:] *anflehen*
positively ['pɔzətivli] *wirklich*
render s.o. attentions ['rendə, ə'tenʃənz] *j-m Aufmerksamkeiten erweisen*
ejaculate [i'dʒækjuleit] *ausrufen*
not yet *noch nicht*
recover [ri'kʌvə] *sich erholen*
astonishment [əs'tɔniʃmənt] *Verwunderung, Erstaunen*
busy o.s. ['bizi] *sich zu schaffen machen*
pile [pail] *Haufen, Stapel*
aside [ə'said] *zur Seite*
uncover [ʌn'kʌvə] *freilegen*
a quantity of ['kwɔntiti] *eine Anzahl von*
building stone ['bildiŋ stəun] *Mauerstein*
mortar ['mɔ:tə] *Mörtel*
materials *Pl* [mə'tiəriəlz] *Ausrüstung*
with the aid of [eid] *mit Hilfe*

---

vigorous ['vigərəs] *tatkräftig*
wall up [wɔ:l] *zumauern*
tier [tiə] *Reihe, Schicht*
masonry ['meisnri] *Mauerwerk*
in a great measure ['meʒə] *in großem Maße, beträchtlich*
worn off [wɔ:n] *von* wear off [wɛə] *nachlassen*
indication [indi'keiʃən] *Anzeichen*
low [ləu] *schwach*
moaning ['məuniŋ] *stöhnend*
obstinate ['ɔbstinit] *hartnäckig*
furious ['fjuəriəs] *wütend, wild*
vibration [vai'breiʃən] *hier: Rasseln*
last [lɑ:st] *andauern, währen*
hearken ['hɑ:kən] *zuhören*
satisfaction [sætis'fækʃən] *Befriedigung, Genugtuung*
cease [si:z] *aufhören mit*
clanking ['klæŋkiŋ] *Gerassel*
subside [səb'said] *sich legen*
resume [ri'zju:m] *wieder aufnehmen*
interruption [intə'rʌpʃən] *Unterbrechung*
nearly ['niəli] *fast*
upon a level with ['levl] *auf gleicher Höhe mit*

in °volume and in strength. I did this, and the °clamourer grew still.

It was now midnight, and my °task was °drawing to a close. I had °completed the eighth, the ninth, and the tenth tier. I had finished a °portion of the last and the eleventh; there °remained but a °single stone to be °fitted and °plastered in. I °struggled with its weight; I placed it °partially in its °destined position. But now there came from out the niche a low laugh that °erected the hairs upon my head. It was °succeeded by a sad voice, which I had difficulty in °recognizing as that of the °noble Fortunato. The voice said—

"Ha! ha! ha!—he! he!—a very good °joke indeed—an excellent °jest. We will °have many a rich laugh about it at the palazzo—he! he! he!—°over our wine—he! he! he!"

"The Amontillado!" I said.

"He! he! he!—he! he! he!—yes, the Amontillado. But is it not getting late? Will not they be °awaiting us at the palazzo, the Lady Fortunato and the rest? °Let us be gone."

"Yes," I said, "let us be gone."

°"*For the love of God, Montresor!*"

"Yes," I said, "for the love of God!"

But to these words I hearkened in vain for a reply. I grew impatient. I called aloud.

"Fortunato!"

No answer. I called again:

"Fortunato!"

°No answer still. I °thrust a torch through the remaining °aperture and let it fall within. There °came forth °in return only a jingling of the bells. °My

ray [rei] *Strahl*
a succession of [sək'seʃən] *eine Reihe* od. *Folge von*
shrill [ʃril] *schrill, gellend*
scream [skri:m] *Schrei*
burst from [bə:st] *dringen aus*
the chained form [tʃeind] *der Gefesselte*
thrust s.o. back [θrʌst] *j-n zurückstoßen*
violent ['vaiələnt] *heftig*
brief [bri:f] *kurz*
hesitate ['heziteit] *zögern*
tremble ['trembl] *zittern*
unsheathe ['ʌn'ʃi:ð] *(aus der Scheide) ziehen*
rapier ['reipjə] *Degen*
grope [grəup] *herumtasten*
instant ['instənt] *Moment, Augenblick*
reassure [ri:ə'ʃuə] *beruhigen*
fabric ['fæbrik] *Gefüge*
reapproach ['riə'prəutʃ] *wieder gehen zu, sich wieder nähern*
yell [jel] *(gellender) Schrei*
clamour ['klæmə] *schreien*
re-echo [ri(:)'ekəu] *hier: nachahmen*
aid [eid] *hier: verstärken*
surpass [sə:'pa:s] *übertreffen*

---

volume ['vɔljum] *Fülle*
clamourer ['klæmərə] *Schreier*
task [ta:sk] *Aufgabe*
draw to a close [drɔ:, kləuz] *sich dem Ende nähern*
complete [kəm'pli:t] *beenden*
portion ['pɔ:ʃən] *Teil*
remain [ri'mein] *bleiben, noch übrig sein*
single ['siŋgl] *einzig*
fit [fit] *einfügen*
plaster in ['pla:stə] *hier: einzementieren*
struggle with ['strʌgl] *sich abmühen mit, Mühe haben mit*
partially ['pa:ʃəli] *teilweise*
destined position ['destind pə'ziʃən] *vorgesehene Lage*
erect the hairs upon s.o.'s head [i'rekt] *j-m die Haare zu Berge stehen lassen*
be succeeded by [sək'si:did] *abgelöst werden von*
recognize ['rekəgnaiz] *erkennen*
noble ['nəubl] *edel, vornehm*

heart grew sick—°on account of the dampness of the catacombs. I °hastened to make an end of my labour. I °forced the last stone into its position; I plastered it up. Against the new masonry I °re-erected the old °rampart of bones. For the half of a °century no °mortal has °disturbed them. °*In pace requiescat!*

joke [dʒəuk] *Witz, Scherz*
jest [dʒest] *Scherz, Spaß*
have many a rich laugh about *noch oft herzlich lachen über*
over one's wine *bei e-m Glas Wein*
await [əˈweit] *erwarten*
let us be gone [gɔn] *laß uns gehen*
for the love of God *um Gottes willen*
no . . . still *noch immer kein . . .*
thrust [θrʌst] *werfen*
aperture [ˈæpətjuə] *Öffnung*
came forth [keim fɔːθ] *von* come forth [kʌm] *herauskommen*
in return [riˈtəːn] *als Antwort*
s.o.'s heart grows sick *j-d fühlt sich elend*

---

on account of [əˈkaunt] *wegen*
hasten [ˈheisn] *sich beeilen*
force s.th. into its position [fɔːs, pəˈziʃən] *etwas mit aller Kraft in die richtige Lage bringen*
re-erect [ˈriːiˈrekt] *wieder errichten* od. *aufschichten, aufstapeln*
rampart [ˈræmpɑːt] *Wall*
century [ˈsentʃuri] *Jahrhundert*
mortal [ˈmɔːtl] *Sterbliche*
disturb [disˈtəːb] *hier: anrühren*
In pace requiescat! *Er ruhe in Frieden!*

Edgar Allan Poe

Edgar Allan Poe, American poet, short-story writer and critic, was born in 1809 in Boston. His parents were itinerant actors. Orphaned at the age of three Poe was taken into the home of John Allan who educated him in schools in England and Richmond, Virginia. Withdrawn from the University of Virginia because of his gambling debts Poe went to Boston, where his first volume of poetry was published anonymously in 1827. He enlisted in the army and later went to West Point Military Academy. But after less than a year he was dismissed for neglect of duty. In the meantime his second volume of poems appeared in 1829.

After years spent in Baltimore and Richmond, where he began to publish stories in magazines, Poe married his fourteen-year-old cousin in 1836 and in 1837 he went to New York. From 1838 to 1844 he lived in Philadelphia where he collected his "Tales of the Grotesque and Arabesque" (published in 1840), and where he edited two magazines. His criticism in these and other journals made him respected and feared. In 1844 Poe moved again to New York. "The Raven and Other Poems" published in 1845 brought him some fame. The appearance of a new collection of short stories in 1846 added even more to this fame. Nevertheless, until his death, Poe struggled against poverty, doing literary hack work and habitually taking to alcohol. In 1849 he was found in the streets of Baltimore, dying in a drunken stupor.

During his lifetime Poe was misunderstood as a man and writer. Literary critics regarded his work as that of a madman. But today, Poe is the most widely read of all American authors of the nineteenth century. Poe is read because he possessed one of the most original imaginations. Never before and rarely since has an author so wholly and impressively captured the special atmosphere which was such a masterful creation of Poe's. His ingenuity and analytic ability was extraordinary. Poe's roots lay in the romantic tale of horror combined with analysis. His stories may be said to fall into two categories: those of horror in which he explored the supernatural and abnormal with gripping suspense; and those of ratiocination which set the standard for the modern detective stories. In these stories each word is in place. The structure of every sentence contributes sharply to the ultimate effect. The climax of horror is reached in a state of genuine excitement.

Poe is the father of the detective story and his influence on the literature of many countries has been enormous. George Bernard Shaw called him "this finest of finest of artists". Sir Arthur Conan Doyle said, "... For those tales have been so pregnant with suggestion, so stimulating to the minds of others, that it may be said of many of them that each is a root from which a whole literature has developed." And Dorothy L. Sayers wrote about him, "... he gave us the working model of the Holmes-Watson combination and of that opposition between the conventional policeman and the unconventional amateur which was later to become a commonplace of detective fiction. He also established the two great formulae for the 'surprise' solution, by way of the unexpected means ('Murders in the Rue Morgue') and the most unlikely person ('Thou Art the Man'), and, in 'The Purloined Letter', pointed the way to the solution achieved by psychological, rather than material, clues." The latter story shows Poe's fine balance of the "intellectual" and the "sensational". "The Mystery of Marie Rogêt" is often thought not only Poe's outstanding achievement in the genre but also one of the best detective stories ever written. But "The Murders in the Rue Morgue" is historically the most important story, since it was the world's first detective story in a modern sense.

It should be recognized, however, that Poe did not think of himself as writing detective stories, the word detective was unknown at the time the first of these stories, "The Murders in the Rue Morgue", appeared. He did not regard these particular stories as of much importance.

In a letter to a friend Poe himself wrote about his stories, "... These tales of ratiocination ... owe most of their popularity to being something in a new key. I do not mean to say that they are not ingenious — but people think them more ingenious than they are — on account of their method and *air* of method ..."

Dorothy L. Sayers

Dorothy L. Sayers was born in 1893 at Oxford. She was educated at Salisbury and at Somerville College, Oxford, where she graduated in medieval literature in 1915. She took up writing as a career and her first novel appeared in 1923. She was probably best known for her Lord Peter Wimsey stories, but her religious plays, in particular "The Man Born to Be King", reached a wide public. She has made a verse translation of Dante's "Divine Comedy". Dorothy Sayers died in 1957.

For her admirers Dorothy Sayers is the finest detective story writer of the twentieth century. In reading her novels one must admire the careful craftsmanship with which they have been made. Her plots are organized with care, the details are often original and carefully researched. She was of the opinion that the stories must possess an "Aristotelian perfection of beginning, middle and end". They must be fair, accurate, interesting and well written, laying all the clues before the reader, and with an unexpected twist towards the end. Of great importance are the logical elements in the unravelling of the mystery.

Dorothy Sayers, tired of reiterated blunt instruments, devoted considerable ingenuity to devising new methods. As early as 1930 one A. Berkeley said, "I am personally convinced that ... the detective story is in the process of developing the novel with a detective or crime interest, holding its readers less by mathematical than by psychological ties. The puzzle element will no doubt remain, but it will become a puzzle of character rather than a puzzle of time, place, motive, and opportunity." Dorothy Sayers wrote in an essay on one of her books, "Gaudy Night", in 1937, "We also took occasion to preach at every opportunity that if the detective story was to live and develop it *must* get back to where it began in the hands of Collins and Le Fanu, and become once more a novel of manners instead of a pure crossword puzzle."

In most of her novels and short stories the actual manner of the murder is not a major feature. Her books are, through clever characterization and description, at the same time novels and stories of character and manners, so that one critic could write about her, "The Wimsey books are for the most part better as novels than as detective novels; they have wit, humour, good character-drawing, and a quality of high seriousness imparted to them by the author's religious sense."

Lord Peter Wimsey, Dorothy Sayers' amateur detective, is a caricature of an English aristocrat, conceived with an immensely snobbish loving seriousness, "yet unique in character and methods". Phrases like the following, where Lord Peter talks to his dentist, are typical examples of his mannerism in speaking: "Oh, some of your whizz-bang business, I suppose ... Jolly old left-hand upper grinder come to bits on me ... Don't be silly, old horse ..." Or he says things like "I'll drop in on you later and we'll have a jolly old pow-wow, what?"

Over the years Wimsey remains essentially unchanged. But after "Busman's Honeymoon", published in 1937, and sub-titled "A love story with detective interruptions", Dorothy Sayers turned away from the hero of whom she had said, "I can see no end to Peter this side of the grave".